D1480970

A NEW PERSPECTIVE ON RACE AND COLOR

A NEW PERSPECTIVE ON RACE AND COLOR

Research on an Outer vs Inner Orientation
to Anti-Black Dispositions

Carroy U. Ferguson

The Edwin Mellen Press
Lewiston•Queenston•Lampeter

Library of Congress Cataloging-in-Publication Data

Ferguson, Carroy U.
  A new perspective on race and color : research on an outer vs.
inner orientation to anti-Black dispositions / Carroy U. Ferguson.
    p. cm.
  Includes bibliographical references and index.
  ISBN 0-7734-8440-X (hardcover)
    1. Prejudices--United States. 2. Racism--United States-
-Psychological aspects. 3. Ethnic relations--Psychological aspects.
4. United States--Race relations--Psychological aspects. 5. United
States--Ethnic relations--Psychological aspects. I. Title
BF575.P9F38   1997
155.8'2'0973--dc21
                                                            97-37726
                                                                CIP

A CIP catalog record for this book is available from the British Library.

        The Edwin Mellen Press   The Edwin Mellen Press
                Box 450   Box 67
        Lewiston, New York   Queenston, Ontario
        USA 14092-0450   CANADA L0S 1L0

                        The Edwin Mellen Press, Ltd.
                        Lampeter, Ceredigion, Wales
                        UNITED KINGDOM SA48 8LT

                    Printed in the United States of America

For my mother, grandmother, and aunt
Inez Ford-Ferguson-Bowden, Evelyn Ford,
and
Jessie Mae McIlwain

TABLE OF CONTENTS

ACKNOWLEDGMENTS

This exploratory study represents a long and challenging process that was completed with the help and support of many people. First, I'd like to thank my brother, Daniel M. Ferguson, Jr., and Mazie Butler Ferguson, for providing me with inspiration and family support. In this light, thoughts of my mother, Inez H. Ford-Ferguson-Bowden, my grandmother, Evelyn H. Ford, and my aunt, Jessie Mae MacIlwain were always primary sources of inspiration who helped me to sustain a sense of motivation and persistence. All were mother figures to me. Love and support were also provided by some dear friends: Nathaniel Mayes, Constantine Comnenou, Maria-Paz Beltran, Fernand Gauthier, Earl Avery, Charles and Toni Hamilton, and Ed Bell.

There were many who contributed directly and sometimes indirectly to the early formation of ideas about this research: Dr. William Ryan, Dr. Marc Fried, Dr. Marianne LaFrance, Dr. Donnah Canavan, Dr. Sandra Sims, Dr. Hauser, and Dr. Ron Nuttal. I want to thank all of those named for providing me with both direct and indirect feedback in helping to shape the foci for the study. Dr. Ed Strickland was an extremely valuable resource person in finding a critical measurement device for one of the variables in the study. My thanks also to Michelle Fagnano, who not only provided emotional support but also played a key role in doing the data collection for the pilot study and for the main study. I'd also like to express my appreciation to Susan Martin, who additionally assisted in the data collection process for the main study. Thanks also to a very supportive employer at the time of the preliminary investigations, Dr. Arne Korstevdt, who put his support into action by serving as one of the judges to score the projective material in this study. Another judge to score the projective material was Rose Lopes.

A special thanks to Dr. Ali Benuazizi, who provided consistent support, guidance, annd encouragement; Dr. Ramsay Liem, who asked many important questions and stimulated the need to be clear; and Dr. William Nasby, who helped stimulate a conceptual approach in regard to data analysis.

Finally, I'd like to acknowledge and express my deepest appreciation and thanks to Lauri Umansky, who not only gave emotional support but who gave untiringly of her time and energy to serve as the primary data collector for the main

study, to serve as one of the judges for the projective material, and to help proof
read this document. Words are inadequate to express how I feel about the nature of
the support that she provided.

Last but not least, I'd like to thank the respondents in both the pilot study
and the main steady for sharing or providing me with information and data. In this
context, a special acknowledgement needs to be made for the Seth-Roberts' book,
The Nature of Personal Reality, a non-empirical work which provided important
and stimulating background for many of the ideas in this study.

ABSTRACT

There were a number of significant findings in this exploratory study about the symbolic link between anti-black disposition and fear of, as well as evaluative attributions (thoughts) about, "the Nature of" the Unconscious. Stimulated by Seth-Roberts' (1972) work, one implied assumption in the study was that the above link was supported or reinforced by the current color coding custom that involves the race-linked colors "black" and "white." That is, the color "black" by custom would carry more fear-related and negative qualities and be linked to "the Black Race" and "the Unconscious" via similarities in affective meanings, particularly the quality "dark." The color "white" by custom would carry less fear-related and more positive qualities and be linked to "the White Race" and "Consciousness" via similarities in affective meanings, particularly the quality "bright." Through these associative links, "the Black Race" may represent or symbolize the "*Un*conscious self," while "the White Race" may represent the "Conscious self" in American culture.

A major finding in the study was that a "black-Black Race-Unconscious" association and a "white-White Race-Consciousness" association were empirically demonstrated and that Outer- and Inner-oriented Caucasians dealt with these associations (rated and clustered them on a Semantic Differential or SD) somewhat differently in regard to Fear and Evaluative dimensions on a SD, particularly in relation to the associative use of the race-linked colors. It was also found that a subset of concepts involving "the Nature of" Satan, the Dreaming State, Death, the Black Race, the Unknown, and the Unconscious tended to have specific affective qualities (meanings) more in common with the color "black," and a subset of concepts involving "the Nature of" God, the Waking State, the White Race, Life, and Consciousness tended to have specific affective qualities (meanings) more in common with the color "white." The "dark-bright" quality appeared to be a significant quality. Further, Outer-oriented Caucasians tended to be more reserved in their expression of Fear *after* certain projective experiences, indicating Fear in regard to the Unconscious. When the Black Race was a factor, however, the Level of Fear increased significantly during the projective experiences, decreased significantly afterwards, but generally did not change from before to after. Black-

White power relations appeared to be a potent issue for most of the Caucasian respondents.

Another major finding in this study was that Outer- and Inner-oriented Caucasians had significantly different attitudes towards Blacks in many instances. That is, Outer-oriented Caucasians had significantly more of an anti-black disposition than Inner-oriented Caucasians. The highest anti-black dispositions tended to occur for both groups in regard to "Ease in Interracial Contact" and "Gradualism." In terms of projection, it was found that both groups *thought* more about (attributed more) "External" conflict/tension in regard to the issue of Black-White interracial intimacy. Despite this, there appeared to be an underlying desire for unity.

The Black Race thus appeared to represent the "Unconscious self" as contrasted with the "Conscious self" for some Caucasians in American society. The findings in this study suggest that race reality continues to be perceived in a distorted manner and that there is a need to examine "associative thought patterns" (or "patterns of associative attributions") and connotations in regard to the meaning of race, color, and "the Nature of" the Unconscious in American culture.

INTRODUCTION

The issue of Fear has received little direct investigation in the study of anti-black prejudice or dispositions. The little research that has been done tends to focus on Fear of retaliation (Donnerstein, Simon & Ditrichs, 1972; Perlman & Oskamp, 1971). The basic premise for this study, which was inspired by Seth-Roberts' *The Nature of Personal Reality* (1972), is that Anti-black Disposition is primarily linked to Fear of (or having Fearful attributions about) "The Nature of the Unconscious." This Fear is associated with the current language customs surrounding black and white that designate racial groups according to a "color code." That is, from a Western and American cultural point of view, the Inner life or Unconscious portions of the Self may have come to represent that dark, Unknown part of the Self which the Caucasian person fears as s/he considers it to have a primitive, chaotic, savage, spontaneous, mysterious, impulsive nature that should be contained and is often repressed. And since the Black Races have dark skin (i.e., black skin or brown skin) and are designated by the language custom via the color code black, which is associated with darkness, they may *symbolize* for some Caucasians the Inner or Unconscious portions of the Self.

Further, it is suggested that in American society or culture the Black Race has represented what some Caucasians think of as the underside of the "proper American citizen," while thinking of themselves as the white, "conscious and objective," more proper side of the Self. Additionally, the orientation is supported and reinforced by the color code which equates the color white with brilliant Consciousness, good, and youth and the color black with the Unconscious, old age, and death. Like Caucasians tended to deal with what they considered to be the primitive, spontaneous, Unconscious Self, then, "Blacks were to be oppressed on the one hand, and yet treated indulgently as children on the other. There was always a great fear that Blacks as a race would escape their bounds–given an inch they would take a yard–simply because the Whites so greatly feared 'the Nature of' the Inner Self and recognized the power that they tried so desperately to strangle within themselves" (Seth-Roberts, 1972, p. 299). The implication is that one's attitude toward the Inner life is significant in the meaning of race and color–that is, in having Anti-black Dispositions.

Several contributors to the personality literature have made a distinction between Inner vs. Outer orientations (Jung, 1935; Adler, 1956; Homey, 1939; Sullivan, 1953), and this stylistic difference may indeed be associated with different attitudes toward Blacks. Murray (1938), in particular, introduced the terms "Intraception" and "Extraception" to describe the differences in tendency or attitude toward "The Nature of the Inner life or Unconscious." He also coined the terms "Exocathection" and "Endocathection" to describe the degree to which an individual was interested in the Inner vs. Outer worlds. The terms refer to the dynamic tension in personality between the ego and the Unconscious and how the individual deals with his Conscious and Inner life experiences.

Sanford et al. (1950) elaborated on the Intraception-Extraception dimension: Intraception (to Murray) stands for "the dominance of feelings, fantasies, speculations, aspirations–an imaginative, subjective human outlook." The opposite of Intraception is Extraception, "a term that describes the tendency to be determined by concrete, clearly observable, physical conditions (tangible, objective facts)." It seems fairly clear, however, that Anti-Intraception, an attitude of impatience with and opposition to the subjective and tender-minded, might well be a mark of the weak ego. The extremely Anti-Intraceptive individual is afraid of thinking about human phenomena because he might, as it were, think the wrong thoughts; he is afraid of genuine feelings because his emotions might get out of control. Out of touch with large areas of his own inner life, he is afraid of what might be revealed if he, or others, should look closely at himself. He is therefore against "prying," against concern with what people think and feel, against unnecessary "talk"; instead he would keep busy, devote himself to practical pursuits, and instead of examining inner conflict, turn his thoughts to something cheerful. ...This general attitude easily leads to a devaluation of the human and an overevaluation of the physical object; when it is most extreme, human beings are looked upon at if they were physical objects to be coldly manipulated–even while physical objects, now vested with emotional appeal, are treated with loving care (p. 235).

It was thought that associated with an Intraceptive (Inner) or Anti-Intraceptive (Outer) orientation might be some significant beliefs, ideas, or constructs that a Caucasian person might utilize to structure his or her experience of the Conscious and Inner life in relation to the Black Race. For example, it was thought that the person's experience of Day (Waking State) and Night (Dreaming State) might be associated with white and black, respectively, based on the person's ideas about light and darkness. The connection here, according to Seth-Roberts (1972), has to do with another association that influences the person–the person's ideas about "The Nature of God and Satan," God being the God of Light and Satan, the Prince of Darkness. In this context, even Life and Death might be viewed in terms of black and white and the value judgments of good and evil– the annihilation of Consciousness being perceived as black and its resurrection as white.

The distinctions regarding ideas about "The Nature of God and Satan" and light and dark apparently have been made at various levels of development of the human species which have to do with the nature of the origin of the present Consciousness (Seth-Roberts, p. 300). These are, therefore, culturally transmitted beliefs or concepts that have been passed on through the centuries in the form of "underground philosophies." For example, in some underground philosophies, black is the symbol of secret knowledge that cannot be found with normal Consciousness or be scrutinized in the light of Day. Here one finds stories of black magicians and legends of the wise old man or woman rising into folklore. In addition, the light of illumination is experienced as white, yet it often appears to delineate the darkness of the soul or to shine in the black of night. According to Seth-Roberts, then, the values about light and darkness are dependent on each other, changing their connotations according to one's beliefs.

Since the Seth-Roberts' work was not research oriented, no empirical evidence was presented to support its propositions. The general purpose of the present research was to study the proposition that Anti-black Disposition is linked to Anti-Intraception (Extraception) or Fear of (or having Fearful attributions about) "The Nature of the Inner life or Unconscious," and to explore the link in "meanings space" (cultural linguistic) between an Inner orientation vs an Outer orientation in terms of what the Black Race may have come to symbolize for many Caucasians via the color code and other associative concepts.

More specifically, the study had two major foci. The first focus was to explore the nature of the link between the "affective meanings," Evaluative connotations, and Fear-related attributions that have come to be associated with the race-linked colors black and white, the race names "The Black Race" and "The White Race," and the concepts or constructs discussed above. Some underlying questions for the first part of the study were: Are there differences in the way in which Outer-oriented Caucasians vs Inner-oriented Caucasians deal with such concepts or constructs as "black," "white," "The Black Race," "The White Race," "The Nature of the Waking State during the Day," "The Nature of the Dreaming State during the Night," "The Nature of God," The Nature of Satan," "The Nature of Consciousness," "The Nature of the Unconscious" (generally as well as more personally), "The Nature of Life," "The Nature of Death," and "The Unknown"? Do Outer-oriented Caucasians polarize and categorize these ideas or constructs in accord with the color-coding custom more than Inner-oriented Caucasians do? How much Fear surrounds the "meaning space" for these ideas or constructs for Outer-oriented Caucasians vs Inner-oriented Caucasians, and is there a significant difference between the two groups?

The second focus for the study was to determine to what extent the Fear Level of Outer-oriented vs Inner-oriented individuals is associated with Anti-black Disposition and to study the issues of projection and the Fear Level of the Outer-oriented vs. Inner-oriented Caucasian person when the Black Race is a factor. The relationship between an Outer orientation vs an Inner orientation and Anti-black Disposition as a set of attitudes was also explored. A central question was, Are there significant differences in how Outer-oriented Caucasians vs Inner-oriented Caucasians manage their Fear surrounding projective experiences and attitude-confrontation experiences involving the Black Race?

LITERATURE REVIEW

Three different sources of literature helped provide the intellectual background for this study. The first source was the literature on the authoritarian personality. The second source was the literature on the color-coding custom regarding racial groups. At a more general level, there was the literature on the history and sociocultural context of Western and U.S. society regarding the meaning of race and color, supported by ideas regarding psychological approaches to understanding human beings and the nature of humanity's inner life or unconscious from a Western perspective.

In the authoritarian personality literature, the "Intraceptive" quality has been found to be more characteristic of the unprejudiced and nonethnocentric person (Adorno et al., 1950). Levinson (1950), for example, in studying personality and ideology found that highly ethnocentric subjects used primarily countercathected defenses and have comparatively narrow and circumscribed egos whereby they constrict fantasy; he noted that this was probably related to the highly ethnocentric subject's emphasis on "sticking to the facts," to their Extraceptiveness, and to their rejection of "imagination" and "emotion." The greater Intraception of the low ethnocentric subjects and the great anti-Intraception of the high ethnocentric subjects were also found to be apparent in their responses to projective questions as well as in material elicited by interviews, the T.A.T., and the F scale (Levinson, 1950, p. 597).

Levinson (1950) also studied ethnocentrism in relation to intelligence and education and found that the intellectual functioning of ethnocentric individuals, even those with above-average I.Q.'s, seemed to be relatively *rigid*, to work better in relation to *things* than to people, to be primarily *Extraceptive*, and to become disrupted when required to deal with more psychological issues, especially those involving personal needs and emotions (Anti-Intraception). Sanford (1950) found similar results in his study contrasting ideologies between two college men and concluded that "one might ask whether such differences in the degree of Intraception, i.e., the inclination to adopt a subjective, psychological, human approach to personal and social problems, do not as a general rule distinguish nonethnocentric from ethnocentric individuals" (p. 44). The relation between ethnocentrism and Extraception (an Outer orientation), then, is well documented and implicitly related to Anti-black Disposition.

The literature on color-coding suggests a basis for Anti-black Dispositions among Caucasians. There is substantial evidence, for example, that the words or color names "black" and "white" carry rather specific evaluative connotations (i.e., negative vs. positive, respectively) or affective meanings. Much anecdotal material is provided in Williams' (1964) study which illustrates the color-coding custom of black as bad and white as good. With Caucasians, white was found to be "good," "active," and "weak" and black was found to be "bad," "passive," and "strong." The reverse polarity of the "weak-strong" affective meaning perhaps represents the relative potency of the color names in "the meaning space" of American culture for these color names. Gergen (1967) argued that "the findings are particularly intriguing inasmuch as they coincide with the popular Western stereotype that Afican Americans are 'strong' but 'lazy' (p. 397). Isaacs (1963) noted that Western and American culture is pervaded with the use of black to symbolize evil and wickedness and white to symbolize goodness and purity. Examples can be found in the most influential literature from the Bible to Shakespeare (Isaacs, 1963), to Poe and Melville (Levin, 1960), in commonly used language (e.g., white lie, snow-white, blacklist, black sheep), and in social customs where brides wear white and mourners dress in black.

A popular and convenient way of referring to racial groups is by color code (e.g., "white" people, "black" people, Indian "red," and Oriental "yellow"), even though it is far from precise (i.e., the skin color of Caucasians is not white, but pinkish-tan; the modal skin color of African American is not black, but brown). Williams (1974) questioned whether this inaccurate use of color names to designate groups of persons influenced the way these groups are perceived and found that the names commonly used to designate Caucasians and African Americans do differ in their general evaluative connotations of goodness and badness. Williams (1965) had earlier demonstrated that for Caucasian respondents the practice of color-coding did influence the meaning of racial concepts such that groups of concepts linked by color code (e.g., White-White people-Caucasian or Black-Black people-Negro) showed a greater similarity in connotative meaning than concepts not so linked (e.g., Red-Oriental people-Chinese).

According to Williams and Morland (1976), there are two major ways in which color is implicated in the meaning of race. First, there is the unavoidable fact that human beings differ in skin color and that color differences constitute highly salient stimuli to the visually oriented Homo sapiens. Secondly, humans show differential attention to the brightness of stimuli during the first days of life (Hershenson, 1964) and make discriminations on the basis of hue by the age of six months (Pagan, 1974). What is the role then of color-coding in the childhood origins of racial attitudes for Caucasian children?

Numerous investigators have found that racial attitudes begin to develop in Caucasian children during pre-school years (eg., Horowitz, 1939; Goodman, 1964; Morland, 1958, 1962). Morland (1958) found that the ability of Caucasian children to recognize individuals by race increased during the ages 3 to 5, with four-fifths of 5-year-olds being able to point out "colored" and "white" persons quite consistently. Morland (1962) found a majority of Caucasian children, aged 3 to 5, expressing a preference for light-skinned playmates and noted that the percent showing this preference increased slightly with age. Goodman (1964) reported varying degrees of racial awareness among Caucasian 4-year-olds: From vague recognition of color differences, to the ability to name racial groups and express consistent preference, to rather adult-like prejudices. Williams and Renninger (1966) thus found that Caucasian children were learning the evaluative meaning of black as bad and white as good during these preschool years when race awareness is developing. In a later study, Williams and Roberson (1967) concluded that race awareness and color connotations do develop concurrently, the latter possibly reinforcing the former.

The above studies suggest that the convenient designation of racial groups by color names may provide children with a general evaluative frame of reference, within which the more specific learnings of prejudice can be easily incorporated.

The findings of Blake and Dennis (1943) are consistent with this notion; they reported that elementary children tended to view Blacks as generally "bad," while high school students viewed Blacks in a more complex way which was similar to adult stereotypes. Morland (1965) in a study comparing race awareness in Northern and Southern children concluded that "regardless of the region the overall effect of American society on very young children has been to influence them to develop a bias for Whites...and that being White is preferable to being Black" (p. 30). A 1971 study by Williams, Tucker and Dunham found some change–but only in the more positive scores of Black college students for the color name "black." The evidence of these early studies, therefore, is that there is some link between the color-coding custom of black as bad and white as good, racial concepts, and race awareness. The studies above suggest that the early learned evaluative connotations and affective meanings help to shape the Caucasian child's and later adult's perceptions about one's self and the Black Race.

Drake (1972) provides a historical background regarding the color-coding custom. He notes that it was only the determination of Europeans to make the concept of "blackness" synonymous with slavery that gave the term "black" its social salience. It was only an insistence upon using anatomical traits to define the status of human beings as inferior that fixed attention upon skin color as a crucial social determinant (p. 308). Prior to the discovery of the New World, the most immediately relevant question was not "Is he black or white?" but "Is he Muslim, Christian, Jew, pagan or infidel?" (p. 311). Subsequently, Social Darwinism, Manifest Destiny, and the White Man's Burden became three of the prevailing ideologies that greatly influenced the institutions and practices of American life both domestically and internationally (Knowles & Prewitt, 1972). With respect to self-concepts or a self-identity, these ideologies provided rationales that linked "black" as bad and inferior and "white" as good and superior to natural evolutionary forces, destiny to control either by natural forces or by Divine Right, and Christian responsibility for helping the poor colored masses to find a better way of life.

The above views were found and supported in religion, the sciences, literature, and law as this country began to struggle with the meaning of race and color differences (Williams & Morland, 1976, p. 3). In the sciences, for example, some early views argued that the Black and White races were separate species, endowed with quite different physical and moral characters (e.g., Morton's *Crania*

Americana). More recent scientific views are that all classification systems have arbitrary features but the black as bad and inferior (negative) and white as good and superior (positive) notion lingers on (e.g., KKK, neo-Natzi groups). For years the country used the law to separate the races on the basis of black and white and still does to some extent (e.g., Woodward's *Strange Career of Jim Crow).* The symbolism reflected in the literature has been noted above (Isaacs, 1963; Levin, 1960). And "in the Judeo-Christian religion, the conflict between the powers of good and evil is portrayed as a struggle between the powers of light and the forces of darkness. On a more personal level, the wayward soul is urged to repent of his black sins, to be cleansed, and to become as 'white as snow'" (Williams & Morland, 1976, p. 39).

Like Seth-Roberts (1972), then, Bastide (1970) argued that the greatest Christian two-part division is that of white and black, that white is used to express the pure, while black expresses the diabolical, that the conflict between Christ and Satan, the spiritual and the carnal, good and evil came finally to be expressed by the conflict between white and black, which underlies and synthesizes all the others (p. 273). Williams (1973) has attempted to study the issue of light and dark and like Seth-Roberts (1972) has suggested that early racial awareness may, in fact, be reflecting primitive feelings about day and night and that children may generalize fear of the dark to skin color. The theory is that very young children have innate preferences for lightness over darkness and such preferences generalize to skin color (as well as to other things). Since the connotative aspects of the color name "black" tends to be associated with symbols of badness, both cultural expectations and linguistic symbolism serve to reinforce racial stereotypes. Offered as support data are findings of all tested cultures preferring light to dark colors. A close link between darkness and blackness is suggested by the work of Palermo and Jenkins (1964), who found that among elementary children "dark" was the word most commonly associated with "black."

A criticism of Williams' theory is that it does not readily explain the attitudes of Black children who have positive associations to dark-skinned parents and loved ones. It has also been found that younger children generalized along the gender dimension whereas older children (9 to 12) generalized on the basis of race (Doke & Rivley, 1972; Katz & Zalk, 1974). It can be argued, however, that during the 1960's African Americans as a race challenged the cultural expectations and linguistic symbolism in redefining themselves, giving the term "black" a more positive connotation for many African Americans, in particular, and for some others in the general population of the country at-large. Further, in common sense terms, significant others are not unknown to the African American (or Black) child; there is no psychological distance that might contribute to a sense of strangeness about the loved one or the skin color. Hence, the need to have these significant others to represent a feared Inner life or Unconscious is minimized. The theory, in any event, does introduce the issue of Fear in terms of how the Caucasian child and later adult may come to feel about him/herself and the Black Races and suggests a link between Fear and how the evaluative connotations and affective meanings for the colors black and white may be inappropriately applied to skin color. When all of this is placed in a religious context as Bastide (1976) does, a link between moral values and the issue of Fear is suggested.

From a Western and American cultural perspective, the experience of Fear in relation to self and others may be linked to prevailing psychological ideas about how to understand "the Self." As Munn (1961) has pointed out, over the last century psychological approaches to understanding mankind began "to see him primarily as an object in nature" (p. 26) with a subjective part of himself that should not (or could not) be looked at because it was too elusive, too difficult to define and measure, and too unsavory. Arising from this history was a characterization of the Unconscious as a portion of the Self against which the Conscious Self (the ego) erects defenses because it finds so objectionable the evil impulses that often get expressed in dreams (Freud, 1916). The affective meaning and symbolism implied then about "The Nature of the Unconscious" is as something dark, mysterious, unknown, evil and bad; hence, the connection to the color name "black."

Seth-Roberts (1972) thus argued that in this society the idea of the Unconscious is equated with darkness or with unknown frightening elements and that it is the Fear in regard to thinking about (making attributions about) the Unconscious as unknown and frightening (i.e., an Extraceptive or Outer-oriented attitude toward "The Nature of the Unconscious") that underlies Anti-black Dispositions as Caucasians project the unacceptable feelings and thoughts in themselves onto African Americans (or the Black Race). That is, in this study it was thought that the Outer-oriented Caucasian in thinking about (making attributions about) the Inner or Unconscious part of himself/herself as harboring these dark, mysterious, unknown, frightening elements is likely to repress his/her emotions, fearing their nature and what s/he might uncover; these repressed emotions then may be projected out onto African Americans (or the Black Race) in line with the associative processes outlined for the study. It was thought that this would be particularly true when, for example, the individual was personally implicated in a tense situation involving the issue of African Americans (or the Black Race) or has to interpret the underlying motives of African Americans (or the Black Race). That is, the Black Race may represent or symbolize the Inner life or Unconsious portions of the Self to him/her as s/he fixes attention on the idea of skin color via associative thoughts (or attributions) about light and dark, white and black, and the other concepts or constructs for the study. The authoritarian personality literature (Adorno et al., 1950) clearly indicates that Anti-Intraception or Extraception (an Outer orientation) is highly associated with projectivity.

In looking at the matter (and meaning) of race and color, there has been little research dealing with the projection theory except as it pertains to projection of sexuality (Halsey, 1946; McLean, 1946; Seidenberg, 1952; Jordan, 1968) and the research findings dealing with the displacement theory give a somewhat confusing picture (Ashmore & DelBoca, 1976). The displacement theory does not specify which group will become the object for displaced aggression, only that it should be visible and relatively defenseless (Zawadeki, 1948). In other words, frustration helps in predicting *when* prejudice will be acted out. It is actually social norms that specify what types of aggressive behavior are allowed and dictate which group is to be scapegoated (Klineberg, 1950). In the context of this study, what the projection theory adds is that the object (the Black Race) represents for the individual unacceptable, inhibited or frightening emotions or characteristics within the person (Poussaint, 1974; Pinderhughes, 1971). Research is sparse but there are accounts which suggest that projection played a role in the original development of anti-black prejudice by the English who first contacted Africans on the African continent (Jordan, 1968) and in the United States (Nash, 1970). Just how it continues to shape Caucasian attitudes towards African Americans (or the Black Race) is not clear due in part to the lack of research. The present study might provide stimulation for additional research dealing with the projection theory and help shed some light on the choice of African Americans (or the Black Race) as the objects of displaced aggression and/or repressed feelings.

In sum, then, the literature on the meaning of race, color, and "The Nature of the Unconscious" shows that the Western and American cultural perspectives, supported by religion, literature, science, law, customs, and psychological assumptions about "The Nature of the Inner life or Unconscious," tend to have an Extraceptive (or Outer-oriented) bias and that Caucasians develop ideas about themselves in relation to the Black Race in this context. For purposes of this study, then, it was thought that the Outer-oriented Caucasian in structuring his/her experience of his/her Conscious and Inner life in U.S. society could easily fix attention on skin color (the physical fact). In so doing, the Black Race may come to represent for him/her what s/he thinks of as the dark, mysterious, unknown, frightening elements that s/he fears s/he might uncover by examining him/herself. It is these elements that may have become equated for him/her with the idea of the Unconscious portions of the Self.

More specifically, it is suggested that the color black, associated with darkness, *symbolically* links the skin color (i.e., black skin or brown skin) of the Black Race with the idea of the Unconscious. Further, in terms of "cultural-linguistic meaning space" for the Outer-oriented Caucasian, similar affective meanings would be evoked within the individual (i.e., something bad or evil, mysterious, primitive, chaotic, etc.) as well as a Fear response. The Outer-oriented person would focus on him/herself in a contrasting manner using the color code white. These associative processes (attributions) then would serve as underpinnings or mediations for when Fear triggers a projection of Anti-black prejudice or Disposition onto African Americans (or the Black Race).

The importance of investigating the suggested links outlined above was to provide some empirical evidence for what the Black Race might symbolize for some Caucasians, further account in part for the intensity of anti-black feelings, and provide further data for *why* some Caucasians might project repressed feelings onto African Americans or the Black Race. Underlying all of this is the central issue of Fear–more specifically, Fear of one's own Self.

HYPOTHESES OF THE STUDY

There were three primary hypotheses for the study:

Hypothesis 1. In regard to Fear and Evaluative responses, Outer-oriented respondents, more so than Inner-oriented respondents, will tend to cluster together the stimulus items "Black," "The Black Race," "The Nature of the Unconscious," "The Nature of the Dreaming State during the Night," "The Nature of Satan," "The Nature of Death," and "The Unknown" in "meaning space" on a Semantic Differential (SD) on the one hand and the stimulus items "White," "The White Race," "The Nature of Consciousness," "The Nature of the Waking State during the Day," "The Nature of God," and "The Nature of Life," on the other. Furthermore:

    a.   These concepts or constructs will be given similar affective meanings, respectively, and will be polarized such that the former subset of concepts will be evaluated more negatively (bad) and the latter subset of concepts will be evaluated more positively (good).

    b.   Generally, there will be a difference in how Outer-oriented repondents vs Inner-oriented repondents deal with (rate on the SD) these respective concepts or constructs in terms of their overall "meaning space" (i.e., salience of the concepts and specific affective meanings for the concepts) and in terms of how they link together these stimulus items in regard to Fear and Evaluative responses.

Hypothesis 2. There is a difference between Outer-orientedness vs Inner-orientedness in regard to events that induce projection. That is, Outer-oriented respondents may experience a higher Level of Fear but will tend to indicate a lower Level of Fear than Inner-oriented respondents since Outer-oriented repondents tend to be more reserved in their emotional expressions. And specifically, when "The Black Race" is made salient as a factor, the Level of Fear will increase for both groups particularly as respondents engage in expressing attitudes about the Black Race.

Hypothesis 3. There is a difference between Outer-orientedness vs Inner-orientedness in regard to Anti-black Dispositions. That is, the repondents' Outer vs Inner orientation is significant in regard to the kind of attitudes they have toward Blacks, their Ethnocentrism and Underlying Feeling States, and how they manifest projective content where the Black Race is a factor.

METHOD

Respondents (Ss)

Respondents were 121 Caucasians, most of whom (81%) were undergraduate students at a northeastern university. Twelve percent of the respondents had completed college and 4% had completed graduate school. There were 47 male and 74 female repondents, ranging in age from 17 to 40. The modal age was 20 years old, and at least 78% of the respondents fell between the ages of 18 and 21. Respondents were recruited from various departments at the university and from the student population at large. Also a small number of repondents (five) were recruited from a Department of Social Service work site in Massachusetts. A pilot study, using a similar recruitment approach, showed no significant differences between the work site repondents and the student respondents in terms of their scores on the key variables of interest in the study.

Besides Sex, Age, and Educational Level, background data for an additional 18 variables were obtained to provide a profile of the sample of respondents (see Table 1). Over half of the respondents were Catholic (59%), while 20% were Protestant (4%), Jewish (3%), Agnostic (3%), and other (10%); twenty-one percent of the respondents had no religious preference or did not identify their religious preferences. The religious beliefs of 72% of the respondents were at least somewhat strong, 60% went to church at least occasionally, and for 71% of the respndents their religious beliefs influenced how they related to others at least some of the time.

Over half of the repondents classified themselves as Upper Class (52%), 27% as Middle Class, and 11% as Lower Middle Class. Sixty percent of the respondents worked either full (21%) or part-time (39%). While 74% of the repondents had personal incomes that fell between $0-6,999, family incomes for 54% of the repondents were above $35,000 and were between $25,000-$34,999 for another 20% of the respondents.

Most respondents (70%) considered themselves to be at least somewhat open in looking at themselves, while another 23% indicated that they were sometimes open and sometimes closed. Nearly all (97%) believed that the Self has both Conscious and Unconscious portions. Two-thirds (67%) remembered their dreams, while the other third (31%) did not. Of those who remembered their Dreams, "The Nature of the Dreams" was Positive for 12% of the respondents, Negative for 28%, mixed Positively and Negatively for 19%, and Neutral in content for 9% of the respondents. Respondents averaged 7.2 hours of sleep per night, the modal number of hours slept per night being 8 and the range of hours slept per night being from 4 to 9 hours. Most respondents (92%) also believed that Intuitions and Hunches were important. Additionally, most respondents saw themselves as either Thinking Types (38%) or Feeling Types (42%); others saw themselves as Intuitive Types (12%) or Sensation Types (4%).

When respondents were asked to identify themselves by "Race and/or Ethnicity," roughly half gave only a Race response (51%), while 17% gave a Race and Ethnicity response and 9% gave an Ethnicity response only. Interestingly, about 43% of the respondents had never had any prolonged contact with a person from another race, 30% had between 1 and 3 years of Other Race Contact, and 12% had less than 1 year of Other Race Contact. Of the 54% who did have some Other Race Contact, the Nature of the Contact was described as "Close" for 32% of the repondents, "Not So Close" for 11%, and "Both Close and Not So Close" for another 11% of the repondents.

Table 1. Summary of Background, Self-Oriented, and Race-linked Profile Measures for All Respondents (Ss), Outer-oriented Repondents (Ss), and Inner-Oriented Responents (Ss)

VARIABLES	All Respondents Ss			Outer-Oriented Ss			Inner-Oriented Ss		
	Freq	Adj. %	Cum %	Freq.	Adj. %	Cum %	Freq.	Adj. %	Cum %
Background									
Sex									
Male	47	39	39	24	40	40	22	37	37
Female	74	61	100	36	60	100	38	63	100
Relgious Preference									
Catholic	71	59	59	35	58	58	36	60	60
Protestant	5	4	63	3	5	63	2	3	63
Jewish	4	3	66	3	5	68	1	2	65
Agnostic	4	3	69	2	3	72	2	3	68
Other	12	10	79	4	7	78	7	12	80
No Preference/No Response	25	21	100	13	22	100	12	20	100
Class									
Lower Class	1	1	1	1	2	2			
Working Class									
Lower Middle Class	13	11	12	5	8	10	8	13	13
Middle Class	33	27	39	19	32	42	14	23	37
Upper Middle Class	63	52	91	29	48	90	33	55	92
Upper Clsss	4	3	94	3	5	95	1	2	93
None of the Above	4	3	98	1	2	97	3	5	98
No Response	3	2	100	2	3	100	1	2	100

Cont. Table 1. Summary of Background, Self-Oriented, and Race-linked Profile Measures

VARIABLES	All Subjects			Outer-Oriented Ss			Inner-Oriented Ss		
	Freq	Adj %	Cum %	Freq	Adj %	Cum %	Freq	Adj %	Cum %
Background (cont.)									
Education									
Completed Graduate School	5	4	4	4	7	7	1	2	2
Completed 4-Year College	15	12	17	3	5	12	12	20	22
Completed At Least 1 Year, Not Graduated	77	64	80	40	67	78	35	58	80
Completed Secondary School	21	17	98	11	18	97	10	17	97
Completed 10th or 11th, Not High School									
Completed Less Than 7 Grades									
No Response	2	2	100	2	2	100	1	2	100
Working Status									
Yes, Full-Time	26	21	21	12	20	20	14	23	23
Yes, Part-Time	47	39	60	25	42	62	22	37	60
No	43	36	96	21	35	97	21	35	95
No Response	5	4	100	2	3	100	3	5	100
Personal Income									
0-$6,999	90	74	74	45	75	75	44	73	73
$7,000-$15,999	6	5	79	4	7	82	2	3	77

Cont. Table 1. Summary of Background, Self-Oriented, and Race-Linked Profile Measures

VARIABLES	Freq	All Subjects Adj %	All Subjects Cum %	Freq	Outer-Oriented Ss Adj %	Outer-Oriented Ss Cum %	Freq	Inner-Oriented Ss Adj %	Inner-Oriented Ss Cum %
Background (cont.)									
Personal Income (cont.)									
$16,000-$24.999	4	3	83	1	2	83	3	5	82
$25,000-$34,999	1	1	83				1	2	83
Above $35,000									
No Response	20	17	100	10	17	100	10	17	100
Family Income									
$0-$6,999	3	2	2	2	3	3	1	2	2
$7,000-$15,999	5	4	7	2	3	7	3	5	7
$16,000-$24,999	13	11	17	8	13	20	5	8	15
$25,000-$34,999	24	20	37	10	17	37	14	23	38
Above $35,000	65	54	91	33	55	92	31	52	90
No Response	11	9	100	5	8	100	6	10	100
Self-Oriented									
Belief That Self Has Conscious & Unconscious Parts									
Yes	117	97	97	58	97	97	58	97	97
No	1	1	98				1	2	98
No Response	3	2	100	2	3	100	1	2	100

Cont. Table 1. Summary of Background, Self-Oriented, and Race-linked Profile Measures

VARIABLES	All Subjects Freq	Adj %	Cum %	Outer-Oriented Ss Freq	Adj %	Cum %	Inner-Oriented Ss Freq	Adj %	Cum %
Self-Oriented (cont.)									
Intuition/Hunches									
Yes	111	92	92	52	87	87	58	97	97
No	6	5	97	5	8	95	1	2	98
No Response	4	3	100	3	5	100	1	2	100
Remember Dreams									
Yes	81	67	67	38	63	63	42	70	70
No	37	31	98	20	33	97	17	28	98
No Response	3	2	100	2	3	100	1	2	100
Nature of Dreams									
Only Positive	14	12	12	5	8	8	8	13	13
Only Negative	34	28	40	14	23	32	20	33	46
Mixed	23	19	59	13	22	53	10	17	63
Neutral	11	9	68	7	12	65	4	7	70
No Response	39	32	100	21	35	100	19	30	100
Openness									
Very Open	51	42	42	20	33	33	30	50	50
Somewhat Open34	28	70	22	37	70	12	20	70	
Sometimes Open,Sometimes Closed	28	23	93	15	25	95	13	22	92
Somewhat Closed	5	4	98	1	2	97	4	7	98
Very Closed									
Don't Know									

Cont. Table 1. Summary of Background, Self-Oriented, and Race-linked Profile Measures

		All Subjects		Outer-Oriented Ss			Inner-Oriented Ss		
		Adj	Cum		Adj	Cum		Adj	Cum
VARIABLES	Freq	%	%	Freq	%	%	Freq	%	%
Self-Oriented (cont.)									
Openness (cont.)									
No Response	3	2	100	2	3	100	1	2	100
Type									
Thinking Type	46	38	38	28	47	47	18	30	30
Feeling Type	51	42	80	20	33	80	30	50	80
Intuitive Type	15	12	93	7	12	92	8	13	93
Sensation Type	5	4	97	3	5	97	2	3	100
No Response	4	3	100	2	3	100	2	3	100
Church-Going Habit									
Regularly	37	31	31	17	28	28	20	33	33
Often	17	14	45	8	13	42	8	13	47
Occasionally	19	16	60	14	23	65	5	8	55
Rarely	29	24	84	14	23	88	15	25	80
Not At All	16	13	98	5	8	97	11	18	98
No Response	3	2	100	2	3	100	1	2	10
Strength of Religious Beliefs									
Very Strong	26	21	21	13	22	22	13	22	22
Strong	33	27	49	15	25	47	17	28	50
Somewhat Strong	28	23	72	15	25	72	13	22	72

Cont. Table 1. *Summary of Background, Self-Oriented, and Race-linked Profile Measures*

VARIABLES	Freq	All Subjects Adj %	All Subjects Cum %	Freq	Outer-Oriented Ss Adj %	Outer-Oriented Ss Cum %	Freq	Inner-Oriented Ss Adj %	Inner-Oriented Ss Cum %
Self-Oriented (cont.)									
Strength of Religious Beliefs (cont.)									
Not At All Strong	15	12	84	6	10	82	9	15	87
Does Not Apply	6	5	89	1	2	84	5	8	95
Don't Know	10	8	98	8	13	97	2	3	98
No Response	3	2	100	2	3	100	1	2	100
Race-Linked									
Race/Ethnicity									
Only Race Used	62	51	51	29	48	48	33	55	55
Race & Ethnicity Used	20	17	68	12	20	68	8	13	68
Only Ethnicity Used	11	9	77	3	5	73	7	12	80
Race & Nationality Used	4	3	80	3	5	78	1	2	82
Ethnicity & Nationality Used	6	5	85	4	7	85	2	3	88
Only Nationality Used	2	2	87				2	3	88
Other	6	5	92	3	5	90	3	5	93
No Response	10	8	100	6	10	100	4	7	100

Cont. Table 1.   Summary of Background, Self-Oriented, and Race-
linked   Profile Measures

		All Subjects			Outer-Oriented Ss			Inner-Oriented Ss	
		Adj	Cum		Adj	Cum		Adj	Cum
VARIABLES	Freq	%	%	Freq	%	%	Freq	%	%
Race-Linked (Cont.)										
Other Race Contact										
Most less than l year	15	12	12	10	17	17	5	8	8
Most 1-3 years	36	30	42	14	23	40	22	37	45
Most 4-6 years	7	6	48	2	3	43	5	8	53
7 years or more	7	6	54	2	3	47	4	7	60
No Contact	52	43	97	30	50	97	22	37	97
No Response	4	3	100	2	3	100	2	3	100
Nature of Race Con-tact										
Close	39	32	32	16	27	27	22	37	37
Not So Close	13	11	43	6	10	37	7	12	48
Both Close & Not So Close	13	11	54	6	10	47	7	12	60
No Response	56	46	100	32	53	100	24	40	10

Operationalizing the Variables

For research purposes, the Outer vs Inner orientation for repondents was
determined by administering questionnaires that measured both the Extraception-
Intraception dimension and the Exocathection-Endocathection dimension in all
respondents. Scores from these two measures were combined to provide an overall
measure of the repondents' tendency toward Extraceptiveness (Outer orientation) vs
Intraceptiveness (Inner orientation). Murray (1963) discussed these dimensions in
his work *Explorations in Personality* and developed a questionnaire to measure each
variable (see discussion below on the questionnaire).

The links in Fear responses, affective meanings, and Evaluative responses and connotations were studied through the use of the Semantic Differential (SD). That is, the Fear responses, the semantic or "meaning space," and the Evaluations among and for the various concepts or constructs were examined in relation to the repondents' Outer orientation vs Inner orientation. In this context, affective meaning refers to the emotional qualities or feelings which stimuli such as words, constructs, ideas, or ideas about phenomena evoke in us, apart from their denotative or "dictionary" meanings. Evaluative responses and connotations, in this context, refer to how positive (good) or negative (bad) the emotional qualities are. The affective meanings of words (linguistic symbolism), constructs, ideas, etc. are important in determining our feelings and behaviors. Williams and Morland (1976) have demonstrated that feeling qualities are associated with groups of people by a particular color-code. They used the Semantic Differential to do so. The Semantic Differential procedure was developed originally in order to provide a method for the assessment of the affective meanings of words, constructs, ideas, and other stimuli (Osgood, Suci, & Tannebaum, 1957). For this study, however, the SD was constructed to also assess the Fear evoked for the stimulus item that was being rated. It was possible, therefore, from the SD procedure to determine both the repondents' average Fear response and average Evaluative response for the concept or stimulus item that was being rated (see SD discussion below). For example, the stimulus item "The Nature of the Unconscious" represents an idea or construct about a phenomenon and it was possible to determine the respondents' average Fear response and average Evaluative response to this stimulus item. The bipolar adjectives used on the SD also provided a way of determining what affective meanings repondents assigned to this stimulus item (e.g., dark-bright; strange-familiar; dirty-clean; profane-sacred; chaotic-organized).

To measure the Level of Fear in relation to projective experiences and attitude-confrontation experiences where the Black Race is a factor, a relatively unobtrusive and brief scale called the Fear Thermometer (Walk, 1956) was used. Respondents were asked to write four Projective Stories, two of which involved the Black Race; respondents rated their Level of Fear or anxiety on the Fear Thermometer *Before* the tasks and then upon completing the tasks rated their Level of Fear for both *During* and *After* the experiences (see discussion on projective measures below). The attitude-confrontation experiences were created by having respondents complete a Multifactor Racial Attitude Inventory (MRAI) (Woodmansee, 1966), which measures racial attitudes on a number of dimensions (see the MRAI discussion below). The Fear Thermometer was used similarly in relation to the MRAI task.

To distinguish the above measures of Fear from trait anxiety or fear, respondents' General Trait Anxiety was determined from their scores on the Fear Survey Schedule (FSS) (Geer, 1965). Trait Anxiety refers to relatively stable individual differences in proneness to view a wide range of situations as threatening and to respond to these situations with elevation in State Anxiety (Spielberger, 1975). State Anxiety (anxiety as an emotional state and in response to a particular situation) is viewed as subjective, consciously perceived feelings of tension, apprehension, and nervousness accompanied by or associated with activation of the autonomic nervous system; it is transient, with fluctuations in intensity over time occurring as a function of the stress perceived by the individual (Spielberger, 1975). In addition to the Fear Thermometer, the Affect Adjective Checklist (AACL) (Zuckerman, 1960) was used to measure repondents' current anxiety levels irrespective of and prior to the specific tasks used to induce projection and attitude-confrontation.

Anti-black Disposition was determined primarily from scores obtained by administering the Multifactor Racial Attitude Inventory (Woodmansee, 1966). Two of eight Projective Questions developed by Levinson (1950) in his study of personality and ideology were also used to look at repondents' Ethnocentrism and Underlying Feeling States as they pertain to the respondents' Outer orientation vs Inner orientation.

A. The Extraceptiveness (Outer)–Intraceptiveness (Inner) Questionnaire

Murray (1963) developed an 80-item questionnaire that sought to distinguish Intraceptive from Extraceptive individuals. Murray also noted that even though an individual may be easily Intraceptive or Extraceptive in disposition, the person may or may not be cathected in a similar manner. As mentioned earlier, he discussed another dimension which he called Exocathection-Endocathection to get at the relative importance to the person of: (1) personal, concrete, physical or social action and (2) fantasy, reflection, imagination, or abstract thought. He indicated that the two variables or dimensions are often confused with one another. Endocathection describes a turning inward (reverie or reflection) and a cathexis of the products of mental activity. This is different from Intraception, for a person may turn outward to engage in practical affairs (Exocathection) with his head full of romantic aspirations, ideals, and intuitions (Intraception); or a person may turn inward (Endocathection) to speculate about the physical properties of Nature (Extraception). Murray thus developed a 20-item sub-questionnaire to measure Endocathection-Exocathection.

For purposes of this study, a 100-item questionnaire was used, which was a combination of the two sub-questionnaires developed by Murray. On Murray's 80-item questionnaire for Extraception-Intraception, 40 of the items dealt with Extraceptive dispositions and 40 items dealt with Intraceptive dispositions. Likewise, on Murray's 20-item questionnaire for Exocathection-Endocathection, 10 items dealt with Exocathective orientations and 10 items dealt with Endocathective orientations. Based on the statistical relationship among Extraception, Intraception, Exocathection, and Endocathection, then, an overall Outer-Inner orientation score was determined for each respondent (see Results section).

B.   The Semantic Differential Measure (SD)

A Semantic Differential (Osgood, Suci, & Tannebaum, 1957) was constructed to provide a measure for (to access) the Fear response, the affective meaning, and the Evaluative response that each respondent gave to each stimulus item. Scales to measure the Understandability of each stimulus item, as well as scales to measure the Activity and Potency of the various concepts or constructs for respondents, were also included. The Understandability scales were based on Nunnally's (1961) study which found the factor; the factor consists of such scales as "strange-familiar" and "mysterious-understandable."

The Fear scales were derived from Block's (1957) study which demonstrated that the Semantic Differential could be successfully utilized as a measure of emotions or attributions about emotions. Hence, the SD scales which rated most highly with the emotion "Fear" were chosen to serve as a subset on the SD constructed for this study. The assumption was that such a construction would provide a measure of the Fear evoked for constructs like "The Nature of the Unconscious" or "The Unknown" and thus would be an indicator which represented a Fear response for what "The Nature of the Inner Self (Inner life or Unconscious)" might "mean" to respondents. To the extent that the description of emotions is a measure of the quality of affective experience, the SD can be utilized as a measure of Fear in this regard (Block, 1957).

Twenty-one stimulus items were rated on 13 scales by respondents. The stimulus items appeared on separate pages, along with the 13 scales. The stimulus items were: "The Nature of Life," "The Nature of Death," "The Nature of Consciousness," "The Nature of the Unconscious," "The Nature of the Unconscious Portions of Me," "The Nature of the Unconscious Portions of the Self," "The Unknown," "The Nature of the Waking State during the Day," "The Nature of the Dreaming State during the Night," "The Black Race," "The White Race," "The Nature of God," "The Nature of Satan," "Black," "White," "Brown," "Red," "Yellow," "People," "Friend," and "Enemy." Included in the list, therefore, were three items about "The Nature of the Unconscious," two race name items, five race-linked colors, two religious items, and three general-people concepts. For this present study, however, the three general-people concepts and the color names other than black and white were not included in the analysis of the results below. This study, therefore, explored fifteen of the stimulus items on the SD.

The 13 scales consisted of four Fear items (passive-active; weak-strong; relaxed-tense; nonfrightening-frightening), six Evaluative items (dark-bright; bad-good; dirty-clean; profane-sacred; relaxed-tense; primitive-civilized), three Understandability items (mysterious-understandable; strange-familiar; chaotic-organized), one Activity item (passive-active), and two Potency items (weak-strong; powerless-powerful). The subset of Fear scales, therefore, contained one Activity item, one Potency item, and one Evaluative item. Osgood et al found that an item might be highly rated on more than one factor. The bipolar adjectives "nonfrightening-frightening" were included as an internal criterion for the other Fear scales. The scales were arbitrarily arranged in the following order on the SD: dirty-clean; sacred-profane; active-passive; strong-weak; mysterious-understandable; powerless-powerful; relaxed-tense; strange-familiar; civilized-primitive; chaotic-organized; good-bad; dark-bright, frightening-nonfrightening.

Since "tense" rates high as a Fear description but rates low as an Evaluative description, the "relaxed-tense" scale was used only as a Fear item for this study. "Strong" rates high both as Fear description and a description of Potency and could thus be used as an item on both subsets of scales. High Fear then meant that the stimulus item was "active," "strong," "tense," and/or "frightening"; Low Fear meant that the stimulus item was "passive," "weak," "relaxed," and/or "nonfrightening." Similarly, Positive meant that the stimulus item was "bright," "good," "clean," "sacred," and/or "civilized"; Negative meant that the stimulus item was "dark," "bad," "dirty," "profane," and/or "primitive." High Understandability meant that the stimulus item was "understandable," "familiar," and/or "organized"; Low Understandability meant that the stimulus item was "mysterious," "strange," and/or "chaotic." And finally, High Potency meant that the stimulus item was "powerful" and "strong"; Low Potency meant that the stimulus item was "powerless" and" weak." "Active" and "passive" were self-evident.

C. The Multifactor Racial Attitude Inventory (MRAI)

A full description of the three extensive studies on which the MRAI is based can be found in Woodmansee and Cook (1965) and Woodmansee (1965). The MRAI is composed of ten 10-item subscales, nine of which are undisguised measures of different aspects of attitudes towards Blacks: (1) Integration-Segregation Policy, (2) Acceptance in Close Personal Relationships, (3) Black Inferiority, (4) Ease in Interracial Contacts, (5) Subtle Derogatory Beliefs, (6) Local Autonomy, (7) Private Rights, (8) Acceptance in Status-Superior Relationships, (9) Gradualism. The tenth subscale, Black Superiority, is included as a potential measure of the tendency to appear falsely equalitarian. Overall, the MRAI provided a measure of various kinds and levels of attitudes on an equalitarian–anti-black continuum. For research purposes, some items were updated with slight modifications and all references to "Negro" were substituted with the words "Black," "Black people," etc.

D. The Projective Measures

As mentioned above, respondents were asked to write four Projective Stories, two of which were race-linked by introducing the Black Race as a factor. More specifically, respondents were given the following four cues, each respectively at the top of a separate blank page: (1) Write a *brief* story involving a person as the boss of employees, (2) Write a *brief* story involving a couple, (3) Write a *brief* story involving a Black person as the boss of White employees, 4) Write a *brief* story involving a Black-White interracial couple. Respondents were instructed to describe what is going on in the story, what people might be *Doing*, *Feeling*, and *Thinking* and how the story ends. The Black Race as a factor was thus introduced to repondents in connection with a projective activity around the themes of power and intimacy, the two most potent themes that appear throughout the literature on race relations.

Two Projective Questions, developed by Levinson (1950), were used to look at respondents' Ethnocentrism and Underlying Feeling States. The Projective Questions were as follows: (1) We all have times when we feel below par. What moods or feelings are the most unpleasant or disturbing to you?; (2) There is hardly a person who hasn't said to himself, "If this keeps up, I'll go nuts!" What might drive a person nuts? Levinson also developed a Scoring Manual for his Projective Questions which connected respondents' responses to Ethnocentrism and Underlying Feeling States. Three judges were employed to use this manual and to score the respondents' responses for this study.

Procedure

Since the primary investigator in the study is Black, three Caucasian female assistants were used for all direct transactions and interactions with respondents. It is fair to say, however, that 95-99% of the transactions and interactions were carried out by only one of the three research assistants. Hence, most respondents were exposed to the same assistant. Respondents were told that they would receive $3.00 as an expression of appreciation for their participation. Basically, repondents reported to a designated room where they were met by the assistant who greeted them, gave them some general instructions, and then handed them a bounded packet of material. The packet contained all of the paper-and-pencil tasks that repondents were to complete. The assistant reminded repondents that they should not skip any of the tasks or any of the items on the various tasks. The assistant then remained in the room, generally sitting at a desk reading until repondents completed all the tasks. When respondents completed the tasks, the assistant thanked them and either gave them a check for $3.00 or informed them that the $3.00 would be sent to them as soon as possible.

The tasks in the packet were organized in a particular way and hence all respondents went through the same process. The first page of the packet consisted of some general introductory instructions. The introductory instructions informed respondents that there were some activities enclosed designed to get some opinions, ideas, feelings, and impressions about different situations and items. They were asked to complete all activities in order and asked not to skip any of the items or activities. Further, respondents were informed that the information would be dealt with in such a way as to maintain confidentiality; they were asked, therefore, to respond *honestly* and *frankly* to the items and activities.

The first task in the packet was a brief one, Zuckerman's (1960) Affect Adjective Checklist. It was included first in order to get a measure of the respondents' State Anxiety or Fear Level for how they felt that day (today). "Today" was defined in the instructions as "from the time you awoke this morning up to the present moment." The next immediate task was The Extraceptiveness (Outer)-Intraceptiveness (Inner) Questionnaire (Murray, 1963). The instructions asked respondents to indicate whether or not each statement was *more* or *less* true for them than it was for the average man or woman of their own age and sex.

Following the questionnaire was the SD procedure, preceded by instructions. Included in the instructions was a general definition for "Unconscious" so that when respondents encountered the term they would be judging the same object or phenomenon. The definition read "'Unconscious' here refers to the parts or portions of the self that one generally is not consciously aware of–the inner, more subjective, not readily conscious parts of the self." Respondents were encouraged to give their first impressions, their immediate "feelings" about the stimulus item. The SD procedure itself, therefore, required respondents to consider a particular stimulus item (e.g., black; The Nature of the

Unconscious) and to describe their feelings about the stimulus item by choosing an appropriate point along a series of 7-point scales, each of which was defined at the extremes of opposite adjectives.

The MRAI followed the SD. The instructions for the MRAI did not mention that the inventory was about the Black Race, only that respondents were to give their opinions by placing a check under agree or disagree on the answer sheet for each statement. Placed immediately after the instructions was Walk's (1956) Fear Thermometer to get a *Before* measure of respondents' Fear Level. Upon completing the MRAI, respondents encountered another page with Fear Thermometers on it that pertained to Fear Levels *During* and *After(now)* for the MRAI task. In the general instructions, respondents were informed that these brief tasks would be encountered.

At this point in the packet, respondents' General Trait Anxiety was measured by the Fear Survey Schedule (FSS). The FSS, which was originally developed by Akutagawa (1956) and modified repeatedly, is the most widely used self-report measure of Fear. Dickson (1975) concluded in a review of behavioral assessment that "the FSS is the most sophisticated assessment instrument in the conventional test format that has been yet developed within the behavioral model" (pp. 360-361). Various factor analytic studies of the FSS, using college students, generally provide evidence of four clusters: (1) fears related to small animals; (2) fears associated with death, physical pain, and surgery; (3) fears about aggression; and (4) fears of interpersonal events. The current study used Geer's (1965) FSS-II version, which had 51 items on it. The instructions for the FSS simply asked respondents to circle for each item the word that most nearly described the amount of Fear that they felt toward the object or situation noted in the item (e.g., Sharp Objects; Death; Dead Bodies). The choices were as follows: (a) None, (b) Very little, (c) A little, (d) Some, (e) Much, (f) Very much, (g) Terror.

The next two general tasks invoved the issue of projection and required respondents to write as opposed to simply reading and making a check mark or circling. Respondents first responded to the Projective Questions. The instructions were straightforward. Respondents were informed that there were no right or wrong answers and that they were simply to respond to both open-ended questions with whatever thoughts, feelings, or impressions that occurred to them. The Projective Stories tasks followed, preceded by instructions. The general instructions informed respondents that they would be given four topics around which to develop stories and that they should use their imagination and first impressions to develop these stories. The Fear Thermometer was used in a similar manner here as with the MRAI, except that on the page immediately following this task Fear Thermometers for *During* and *After(now)* for each story were included.

The final task that respondents completed in the packet was a three page Background Data Form where they marked appropriate spaces or gave brief written responses. The Background Data Form provided information about 21 profile measures: (1) Sex, (2) Age, (3) Religious Preference, (4) Race & Ethnicity,(5) Belief that the Self has Conscious and Unconscious portions, (6) Openness, (7) Remember Dreams, (8) Nature of Dreams, (9) Importance of Intuition/Hunches, (10) Type (i.e., Thinking Type, Feeling Type, Intuitive Type, Sensation Type), (11) Church-going Habit, (12) Class, (13) Working or not, (14) Strength of Religious Beliefs, (15) Other Race Contact, (16) Nature of Race Contact, (17) Personal Income, (18) Family Income, (19) Influence of Religious Beliefs in Relating to Others, (20) Education Level, and (21) Sleep Habits.

RESULTS AND DISCUSSION

The first step in testing the hypotheses of this study was to differentiate the respondents on the basis of their Outer vs Inner orientations. The results of a factor analysis indicated that the combined Extraception-Intraception and Exocathection-Endocathection dimensions on the Extraceptiveness (Outer)-Intraceptiveness (Inner) Questionnaire constituted a single Factor and hence could be used as a measure to differentiate respondents (see Table 2). Scores obtained from the 40 Extraceptive items, the 40 Intraceptive items, the 10 Exocathective items, and the 10 Endocathective items constituted the variables for the factor analysis.

Table 2 shows the correlations among the four variables (the different sides of the two continua) and the summary results of the factor analysis (i.e., profile measures, factor matrix, communalities, etc.). While the correlation coefficients were not high, they did illustrate the way in which the different sides of the two continua relate. Intraception was thus positively related to Endocathection ($r = .49$), but negatively related to Extraception ($r = - 41$), and Exocathection ($r = -.11$). Extraception was positively related to Exocathection ($r = .59$), but negatively related to Intraception and Endocathection ($r = -.36$); Endocathection and Exocathection were negatively related ($r = -.34$). On the whole, respondents tended to lean toward Intraceptive tendencies and were relatively balanced as far as being cathected inwardly vs. outwardly. Nevertheless, the Extraception variable had more in common with the other variables that constitute the Extraceptiveness (Outer orientedness)-Intraceptiveness (Inner orientedness) Factor.

Given the above associations, the following formula was used to calculate an overall Outer-Inner orientation score for each respondent: overall Outer-Inner orientation score = Extraception minus Intraception minus Endocathection plus Exocathection. The maximum score possible for the most Outer-oriented

respondents was 250 and the minimum score possible for the most Inner-oriented
respondents was -250. To actually classify respondents into an Outer-oriented
group and an Onner-oriented group, the median for the overall Outer-Inner
orientation scores was determined (median = -30). Respondents with scores above
the median score were defined as "Outer-oriented," while respondents with scores
below the median were defined as "Inner-oriented." Each group, then, included 60
respondents. The actual range of overall Outer-Inner orientation scores for the
sample as a whole was 179, with a maximum score of 44 and a minimum score of
-135. It should be noted, then, that this was a somewhat negatively skewed sample
(skewness = -29). That is, the overall Outer-Inner orientation scores tended to
cluster around the Inner orientation (X = -32.67).

**Table 2.   *Summary of Correlations and Factor Analysis Results for
Different Measures of Intraception, Extraception,
Endocathection, and Exocathection.***

A.   Correlation Coefficients

	Intraception	Extraception	Endocathection	Exocathectior
Intraception	1.00	-.41	.49	-.11
Extraception		1.00	-.36	.59
Endocathection			1.00	-.34
Exocathection				1.00

B.   Summary of Profile Measures (Means, Standard Deviations) and Factor Analysis Results

| | | | Factor Matrix | |
| | Means | SD | With Iteration | Communality |
Variables				
Intraception	122.71	17.51	-.52	.27
Extraception	88.53	18.10	.80	.65
Endocathection	27.16	6.55	-.59	.35
Exocathection	28.67	6.74	.57	.33

Table 1 compares Outer-oriented respondents and Inner-oriented respondents on several background measures (see Table 1 under Method section, Respondents). As an exploratory study, levels of significance were established at p < .05 and p < .10. Future research might and perhaps should use more stringent criteria. Tests of significance (t-tests) between Outer-oriented respondents and Inner-oriented respondents showed that, at p < .10, the two groups were significantly different in their Belief that Intuition and Hunches are Important (Outer, X = 1.09, SD = .94; Inner, X = 1.02, SD = .13; t = 1.71, p < .09). That is, Inner-oriented respondents (97%) were somewhat more inclined to believe that intuition and hunches are important than Outer-oriented respondents (87%). Similarly, a difference between Outer-oriented respondents and Inner-oriented respondents nearly approached statistical significance with regard to the Nature of Dreams (Outer, A = 2.56, SD = .94; Inner, X = 2.24, SD = .88; t = 1.61, p < .11). That is, while the Nature of the Dreams for both groups of respondents tended to be relatively negative and mixed, the Nature of Dreams for Inner-oriented respondents was slightly more Negative (33%) and slightly less Mixed (17%) than for Outer-oriented respondents (i.e., Negative = 23%; Mixed = 22%). Additionally, while the percentages were low, the Nature of Dreams for Inner-oriented repondents was also slightly more Positive (13%) and slightly less Neutral (7%) than for Outer-oriented repondents (i.e., Positive = 8%; Neutral = 12%). It might not be possible to make too much of this, except in the sense of a possible slight tendency. That is, affectively, Inner-oriented respondents may have a slight tendency to experience "the Nature of" their dreams somewhat more intensely than Outer-oriented respondents.

In this study, "Negative" meant that the remembered dreams were confusing and made little sense, were recurring dreams or were nightmares; "Mixed" meant that the remembered dreams were Negative and/or "Positive" (i.e., clear and instructive) and/or Neutral; "Neutral" meant that the remembered dreams were given little attention by respondents or that repondents did not know what to think about their dreams. Though not a statistically significant difference, slightly more Inner-oriented respondents (70%) tended to remember their dreams than Outer-oriented repondents (63%) did.

While not significant statistically, some other subtle distinctions were observed between Outer-oriented respondents and Inner-oriented respondents. For example, while 70% of both groups considered themselves to be at least "Somewhat Open" to looking at themselves, half of the Inner-oriented respondents (50%) considered themselves to be "Very Open" as compared to about a third of the Outer-oriented respondents (33%). Further, while 80% of both groups saw themselves as either "Thinking Types" or "Feeling Types," about half of the Outer-oriented respondents saw themselves more as Thinking Types (47%) than as Feeling Types (33%), whereas half of the Inner-oriented respondents saw themselves more as Feeling Types (50%) than as Thinking Types (30%). Also, slightly more Outer-oriented respondents (65%) than Inner-oriented respondents (55%) tended to go to church at least occasionally. Finally, in regard to "Other-Race Contact," more Outer-oriented respondents (50%) than Inner-oriented respondents (37%) had never had any prolonged contact with a person from another race. Of the 47% Outer-oriented respondents who did have some Other-Race Contact, the Nature of the Contact was described as "Close" for 27% of these respondents, "Not So Close" for 10%, and "Both Close and Not So Close" for 10%. Of the 60% Inner-oriented repondents who had some other-race contact, the Nature of the Contact was described as "Close" for 37% of these respondents, "Not So Close" for 12%, and "Both Close and Not So Close" for 12%.

It should be noted at this point that the general Ss population, both Outer-oriented resondents and Inner-oriented respondents, tended to be somewhat fearful overall. That is, the General Trait Anxiety or Fear and State Anxiety or Fear for both Outer- and Inner-oriented respondents tended to be somewhat higher than average. According to Geer (1965), the average score for men on the FSS (Fear Survey Schedule) for General Trait Anxiety is 75.78 with a standard deviation of 33.84; the average score for a woman on the FSS is 100.16 with a standard deviation of 36.11. In this study, the average score for all Ss on the FSS was 175.43 with a standard deviation of 38.41; the average score for Outer-oriented respondent on the FSS was 175.05 with a standard deviation of 34.60; and the average score on the FSS for Inner-oriented respondents was 176.65 with a standard deviation score of 41.93. Statistically, then, there was no significant difference between Outer- and Inner-oriented respondents in terms of General Trait Anxiety.

In terms of the State Snxiety of the Ss in this study, the Level of Fear tended to be moderately high as measured by the AACL (Affect Adjective

Checklist). According to Zuckerman (1960), the possible range of scores on the AACL is O to 21, 0 to 7 indicating a relatively low level of anxiety, 8 to 14 indicating a relatively moderate level of anxiety, and 15 to 21 indicating a relatively high level of anxiety. In this study, the average score for all Ss on the AACL was 8.22 with a standard deviation of 4.31; the average score for Outer-oriented respondents on the AACL was 7.80 with a standard deviation of 4.09; and the average score on the AACL for Inner-oriented respondents was 8.65 with a standard deviation of 4.53. Though Inner-oriented respondents tended to indicate a slightly higher level of State Anxiety before engaging in the various tasks for this study, no significant difference was found between Outer- and Inner-oriented respondents statistically.

Overall, then, Inner- and Outer-oriented respondents in this study tended to be fairly similar to each other in terms of Sex, Age, the Use of Race and/or Ethnic Labels, Religious Preferences, the Belief that the Self has Conscious and Unconscious parts, Class, Work, Strength of Religious Beliefs, the Influence of Religious Beliefs in Relating to Others, Personal and Family Incomes, Sleep Habits, General Trait Anxiety and Level of Education. There were, however, certain subtle differences between Outer- and Inner-oriented respondents in terms of the importance that each group attached to Intuition and Hunches, the tendency to Remember their Dreams, the Nature of their Dreams, their respective Openness, the description of themselves as Thinking vs Feeling Types, their Church-going Habits, their Indicated State Anxiety, their Other-Race Contact, and the Nature of their Other-Race Contact.

As the results of the study show below, these subtle differences between the two groups led to findings of significant differences and effects in many instances in regard to the hypotheses for this exploratory study. With a larger sample size and using the top twenty-five per cent of each group for comparative purposes, it might be anticipated that even more dramatic results would occur.

Clustering Patterns for Proposed Race-linked Concepts on Fear and Evaluative Dimensions

A series of factor analyses were used to examine how the 15 concepts or constructs for the study clustered in regard to both the Fear and Evaluative dimensions in semantic or "meaning space" on the SD. Hypothesis 1 predicted that for Outer-oriented respondents, on both of these dimensions, stimulus items involving the color black, the Black Race, and "The Nature of" the Unconscious, the Dreaming State (night), Death, Satan, and the Unknown would cluster together and stimulus items involving the color white, the White Race, and "The Nature of" Consciousness, the Waking State (day), Life, and God would cluster together. Hypothesis 1 also predicted that for Inner-oriented respondents these respective clustering patterns in regard to Fear and Evaluation would not be as pronounced. Furthermore, Hypothesis 1-b predicted that in regard to Fear and Evaluation, Outer-oriented respondents and Inner-oriented respondents would link together these concepts or constructs in different ways in "meaning space."

In general, overall clustering patterns that included *all* of the respective subsets of stimulus items did not occur in the exact manner predicted. That is, no single Factor structure was found which included all of the stimulus items as hypothesized for Outer-oriented respondents. In fact, a factorially complex picture emerged for both Outer-oriented respondents (five Factors) and Inner-oriented respondents (five Factors) on both the Fear and Evaluative dimensions. Despite this, some of the predicted links (as well as some understandable, unanticipated links) were observed on some of the Factors for both Outer- and Inner-oriented respondents. For Outer-oriented respondents, in regard to both race name stimulus items, "The Black Race" and "The White Race," some of the predicted links tended to be more pronounced for them in an Evaluative context. For Inner-oriented respondents, while some of the predicted links in regard to "The Black Race" tended to be more pronouced for them in the context of Fear, the links involving "The White Race" did not include the color "white." For example, a "black-Black Race-Unconscious" association was more pronounced for Outer-oriented respondents in an Evaluative context, when the priority focus (highest loading on the Factor) was the issue of "The Nature of Death," but was more pronounced for Inner-oriented respondents in the context of Fear when the priority focus was "The

Unknown." A "white-White Race-Consciousness" association was more pronounced for Outer-oriented respondents in an Evaluative context, when the priority focus was the color "white," but Inner-oriented respondents only maintained a "White Race-Consciousness" association in both Fear and Evaluative contexts without a significant connection to the color "white." Other stimulus items were also significantly linked to the above associations. Overall, then, Outer- and Inner-oriented respondents did tend to link together the concepts in somewhat different ways in "meaning space." A full discussion of the various Factors follows.

The Factors that were found in this study may be looked at in terms of different associative links or thought patterns or patterns of associative attributions at play in the culture. For interpretive purposes, a "high loading" was .66 and above, a "moderately high" loading was .46 to .65, "some loading" was .30 to .45, "leaning toward some leading" was .25 to .29, a "low loading" was .10 to .24, and a "very low loading" was below .10. Also, each Factor can be said to have had a priority focus, determined by the highest loading item on the factor. Further, the Factors exhibited at least a tendency toward bipolarity, which approached a significant level in the case of some Factors. A true bipolar Factor is one that has substantial positive and negative loadings, which amounts to saying that the positive and negative aspects of the same thing are being measured (Kerlinger, 1967, p. 668). Positive and negative simply refer to directions and not to a quantitative difference. So, while it was found that the Outer vs Inner orientation did make a difference, generally, in terms of what items loaded highest, the relationship between a person's orientation and the clustering of all of the stimulus items on the Fear dimension was much more complex than was predicted.

Table 3 compares the clustering of the Factor loadings of the 15 concepts or constructs on the Fear dimension for Outer-oriented respondents and Inner-oriented respondents. Factor I, for Outer-oriented respondents, then, indicated that in the context of Fear, as thoughts (Fears or Fearful attributions) about a personalized Unconscious are linked directly to thoughts (Fears or Fearful attributions) about "The Nature of" Consciousness, the Waking State, and the Unknown, it seems to represent bipolarly the same thing as fearing (or having Fearful attributions about) "The Nature of" God for them. Here, an "Unconscious-Unknown" association is directly linked to a "Consciousness-Waking State" association and these

Table 3. Clustering of the Factor Loadings of the Fifteen Concepts on the Semanitic Differential: Comparison of Outer-Oriented Respondents and Inner-Oriented Respondents on the Fear Dimension.

FACTORS	Outer-Oriented Ss CONCEPTS	Inner-Oriented Ss CONCEPTS
Factor I		
High +	Unconscious/Me(.76)	Unconscious/Me(.87)
	Unconscious/Self(.70)	Unconscious/Self(.72)
Mod. High +	Consciousness(.55)	Unconscious(.62),
	Waking/Day(.53)	Dream/Night(.51)
Some +	Unknown(.31)	Waking/Day(.38), Death (.34)
Low +	Unconscious(.22),	Satan(.23), God(.19),
	White Race(.21),	Unknown(.14),Black
	Dream/Night(.21)	(.14), Life (.12)
	Black(.17), Satan(.16),	
	Black Race(.16)	
Very Low +	Death(.04)	White Race(.06), Cons-sciousness(.03)
Leans Toward Some -	God(-.27)	
Low -	Life(-.12)	
Very Low -	White(-.02)	White(-.03), Black Race (-.01)
Factor II		
High +		Unknown(.84)
Mod. High +	Death(.59), Black Race (.50), God(.49)	Black(.65), Black Race (.50)
Some +	Dream/Night(.44), Black (.43), White Race(.37)	Unconscious(.36), Dream/Night(.31) Satan(.30)

Table 3 (cont.) *Clustering of Factor Loadings of the Fifteen Concepts on the Fear Dimension for Outer vs. Inner-Oriented Respondents*

<u>**Factor II**</u> (cont.)

Leans Toward Some +	Waking/Day(.25)	
Low +	Consciousness(.21), Satan(.14), Unconscious (.11), Unknown(.10)	Unconscious/Self(.22), Death(.21), Life(.15), God(.13), White Race(.12) Consciousness(.05)
Very Low +	Unconscious/Me(.09), Life(.06), Unconscious/ Self(.04)	
Low -		Waking/Day(-.17) Unconscious/Me(-.11)
Very Low -	White (-.09)	

<u>**Factor III**</u>

High +	Satan(.77)	White Race(.80), Consciousness(.68)
Mod. High +	Unknown(.59)	
Some +	Life(.43), Black(.32), Consciousness(.31)	
Low +	Unconscious/Self(.14), Unconscious(.13), Unconscious/Me(.13), Black Race(.12), Dream/Night (.11)	Satan(.20), Life(.17), Waking/Day(.16), Unconscious/Me(.14), Black Race(.12), Unconscious (.11)
Very Low +	God(.08), Death(.07) White Race(.001)	Black(.08), White(.02), God(.02)

*Table 3 (cont.)   Clustering of Factor Loadings of the Fifteen
Concepts on the Fear Dimension for Outer vs. Inner-Oriented
Respondents*

Factor III (cont.)

Leans Toard Some -   Dream/Night(-.29)

Very Low -   White(-.09), Waking/Day   Unconscious/Self(-.07),
                        (-.08)   Unknown(-.07), Death
                                                    (-.03)

Factor IV

High+   Unconscious(.69)

Mod. High +   Dream/Night(.51)   Life(.47)

Some +   Unconscious/Self(.36),   Black(.44)
                       Unconscious/Me(.34),
                       God(.33), Life(.30)

Leans Toward Some +   Death (.26)

Low +   Unknown(.23), Black   Unconscious(.23),
                       Race(.13)   Waking/Day(.17)
                                                   Consciousness(.14)

Very Low +   White Race(.05), Death   Unconscious/Me(.01)
                       (.05), Black(.04), Satan
                       (.003)

Some -   White(-.41)

Low -   Satan(-.22), Unknown
                                                   (-.20), White Race(-.19),
                                                   God(-.16)

Very Low -   Consciousness(-.06),   Dream/Night(-.09),
                       Waking/Day(-.05), White   Unconscious/Self(-.09),
                       (-.04)   Black Race(-.02)

Table 3 (cont.) Clustering of Factor Loadings of the Fifteen Concepts on the Fear Diminsion for Outer vs.Inner-Oriented Respondents.

Factor V

High +	White(.77)	
Mod. High +		Life(.61), God(.42)
Some +	God(.42), Unknown(.36)	
Leans Toward Some +		
Low +		Unconscious/Me (.17), Dream/Night(.16), Unconscious/Self (.15), Satan(.13), Black Race (.12), Unknown(.10), Unconscious(.10)
Very Low +	Death(.09), Waking/Day (.04), Unconscious(.01), Unconscious/Me(.005)	White(.02)
Low -	Black(-.23), Satan(-.16), Consciousness(-.16)	Death(-.23)
Very Low -	White Race(-.09), Black Race(-.06), Unconscious/ Self(-.05), Life(-.02), Dream/Night(-.002)	Black(-.09), Waking/ Day(-.03), White Race (-.008)

associations are bipolarly linked to the concept of God. Factor I, for Inner-oriented Ss, indicated that in the context of Fear, as thoughts (Fears or Fearful attributions) about "The Nature of the Unconscious" in personal and general terms are linked directly to thoughts (Fears or Fearful attributions) about "The Nature of" the

Dreaming State and the Waking State, thoughts (Fears or Fearful attributions) about the Nature of Death become significantly associated. Here, an "Unconscious-Dreaming State-Death" association is directly linked to "The Waking State." On both of these Factors, the priority focus (i.e., highest loading item) was "The Nature of the Unconscious Portions of Me" (high +), followed by "The Nature of the Unconscious Portions of the Self" (high +). The race-linked colors ("black" and "white") and the race names ("The Black Race" and "The White Race") did not load significantly on the respective Factors for either group. For both groups, however, the colors did show a slight bipolar tendency (i.e., for both groups "black" loaded low + and "white" loaded very low-), and only for Inner-oriented respondents did the race names show a slight bipolar tendency (i.e., "The White Race" loaded low + and "The Black Race" loaded very low -).

Factor II, for Outer-oriented respondents, indicated that in the context of Fear, thoughts (Fears or Fearful attributions) about race (i.e., "The Black Race" more significantly than "The White Race"), religion (i.e., the concept of God), color (i.e., black), the Dreaming State and probably Waking State fears or fearful attributions may become salient issues for them as they scare themselves when thinking about (fearing or having Fearful attributions about) "The Nature of Death." Of particular interest, here, is a fairly strong "Death-Black Race-Dreaming State-black" association and how Outer-oriented respondents directly linked this association to a "God-White Race-Waking State" association. For Inner-oriented respondents, Factor II indicated that in the context of Fear, an "Unknown-black-Black Race-Unconscious-Dreaming State-Satan" association occurred when the priority focus was "The Unknown." That is, except for the item "The Nature of Death," many of the predicted associative links (thoughts or Fears or Fearful attributions) tended to occur for Inner-oriented respondents as they feared "The Unknown." Interestingly, then, when all of the item loadings were considered, the clustering patterns that were predicted for Outer-oriented respondents tended to be more pronounced for Inner-oriented Ss on this Factor. As indicated, with respect to these two Factors, the priority focus for Outer-oriented respondents on Factor II was "The Nature of Death" (moderately high +), while the priority focus for Inner-oriented respondents on Factor II was "The Unknown" (high +).

On Factor III for Outer-oriented respondents, in the context of Fear, a "Satan-Unknown-black" association was directly linked to a "Life-Consciousness" association. On Factor III for Inner-oriented respondents, in the context of Fear, a "White Race-Consciousness" association was slightly linked bipolarly to "The Nature of the Dreaming State." That is, these two Factors indicated, respectively, that in the context of Fear, Outer-oriented respondents apparently associated the concept of Satan (or ideas about "The Nature of Satan") with their thoughts (Fears or Fearful attributions) about the Unknown aspects of "The Nature of Life," which they may experience as the black side of Consciousness. Inner-oriented respondents, on the other hand, apparently juxtapose bipolarly Fears (or Fearful attributions) related to "The Nature of" their Consciousness and their Dreams when thinking about (fearing or having Fearful attributions about) their self-reference group. In other words, it is as if the Fears (or Fearful attributions) associated with "The Nature of the Dreaming State" for Inner-oriented respondents are somewhat represented by (means the same thing as) the self-reference group (i.e., "The White Race") linked directly to "The Nature of Consciousness" in the context of Fear. The third priority focus for Outer-oriented respondents, here, in regard to Fear was "The Nature of Satan" (high +); the third priority focus for Inner-oriented respondents in regard to Fear was "The White Race" (high +). The race name items and the color "white" (very low -) did not load significantly on Factor III for Outer-oriented respondents, though "The Black Race" (low +) was weighted slightly higher than "The White Race" (very low +) and the race-linked colors did show a slight bipolar tendency. The race-linked colors (both very low +) and "The Black Race" (low +) did not load significantly on Factor III for Inner-oriented respondents.

Factor IV, for Outer-oriented respondents, indicated that in the context of Fear, these respondents, in thinking about (fearing or having Fearful attributions about) "The Nature of the Unconscious" in general, not only directly associated their thoughts (fears or fearful attributions) about "The Nature of" their Dreams and a personalized Unconscious, but also directly associated their thoughts (Fears or Fearful attributions) about religion (i.e., the concept of God) and "The Nature of Life." An "Unconscious-Dreaming State" association, then, is linked directly to a "God-Life" association. Factor IV, for Inner-oriented respondents, indicated that these respondents, in thinking about (fearing or having Fearful attributions about) "The Nature of" Life and probably Death, in the context of Fear, associated the race-linked colors in such a way that "black" gets directly associated and "white" gets bipolarly associated. A bipolar "Life-white" association, then, is linked to a direct "Death-black" association here. The race-linked colors and race names did not load significantly on Factor IV for Outer-oriented respondents, though the colors ("black," very low +; "white," very low -) did show a slight bipolar tendency and "The Black Race" (low +) was weighted slightly higher than "The White Race" (very low +). The race names did not load significantly on Factor IV for Inner-oriented respondents, though interestingly both loaded bipolarly along with the color "white." "The White Race" (low -) was weighted slightly higher than "The Black Race" (low -) on this factor. The priority focus for Outer-oriented respondents on Factor IV in regard to Fear was "The Nature of the Unconscious" in general (high +); the priority focus for Inner-oriented respondents on Factor IV in regard to Fear was "The Nature of Life" (moderately high +).

Finally, on Factor V in regard to Fear for Outer-oriented respondents, the link between "white" and "God" was demonstrated, as well as an unanticipated, but understandable link between "God" and "The Unknown." That is, a great deal of religious dogma teaches that one must fear (or have Fearful attributions about, probably in terms of Potency) a great, Unknown, impersonal, Almighty God. For Inner-oriented respondents, in terms of Fear, the fifth Factor suggested that as these respondents Fear (or have Fearful attributions about) Life, their Fear of (or Fearful attributions about) "The Nature of God" gets associated. That is, a "Life-God" association was significant here for Inner-oriented respondents.

Table 4 shows the clustering patterns that emerged on the Evaluative dimension for Ss. As indicated above, a factorially complex picture was also found here for Outer-oriented respondents (five factors) and Inner-oriented respondents (five Factors). As with the Fear dimension, the Factors tended to have at least some bipolar quality to them, with a few Factors being relatively significant in this regard. Here, each Factor may be reflecting something about associative thought patterns or patterns of associative attributions that may be at play in regard to value judgments that are made in an Evaluative context.

On the first Factors that emerged for both Outer- and Inner-oriented respondents in an Evaluative context, the "Unconscious-Dreaming State" association was clearly evident. Outer-oriented respondents, however, linked this association directly to "The Nature of Death," while Inner-oriented respondents linked this association directly to "The Unknown." Further, for the Outer-oriented

Table 4. Clustering of the Factor Loadings of the Fifteen Concepts on the Semantic Differential: Comparison of Outer-Oriented Respondents and Inner-Oriented Respondents on the Evaluative Dimension

FACTORS	Outer-Oriented Ss CONCEPTS	Inner-Oriented Ss CONCEPTS
Factor I		
High +	Unconscious/Me(.77), Unconscious/Self(.75) Unconscious(.70)	Dream/Night(.76), Unconscious/Me(.72) Unconscious(.68), Unconscious/Self(.67)
Some +	Dream/Night(.44)	
Leans Toward Some +	Death(.25)	Unknown(.27)
Low +	Satan(.23), Waking/Day (.22), Life(.22), Un-known(.22), Black Race (.21), Consciousness (.18), Black(.16), White Race(.10)	Life(.19), Consciousness (.17), Black Race(.16)
Very Low +	God(.09)	White(.09), Death(.08), Waking/Day(.07), God (.05), White Race(.02), Black(.02)
Low -	White(-.11)	
Very Low -		Satan(-.09)
Factor II		
High +	White(.71)	Death(.75)
Mod. High +	Consciousness(.60), White Race(.53)	Black Race(.57), Unkown(.55)
Some +	Waking/Day(.38), Life(.38)	God(.44), Life(.42), Waking/Day(.38)

*Table 4 (cont.).   Clustering of Factor Loadings of the Fifteen
Concepts on the Evaluative Dimension for Outer vs. Inner-
Oriented Respondents*

Factor II (cont.)

Leans Toward Some +	Unconscious(.28)	Unconscious(.28), Unconscious/Self(.25)
Low +	Unconscious/Self(.13), Death(.12)	Unconscious/Me(.19), Black(.13)
Very Low +	Unknown(.06), Unconscious/Me(.02)	Dream/Night(.01)
Some -	Dream/Night(-.31)	
Low -	Satan(-.22), Black Race (-.21), Black(-.18)	
Very Low -	God(-.06)	White Race(-.08), Satan (-.08), White(-.05), Consciousness(-.03)

Factor III

High +	Death(.68)	White Race(.80)
Mod. High +	Black(.61), Black Race (.51)	Consciousness(.61), Life (.53), Unconscious/Me (.46)
Some +	Waking/Day(.42) Unconscious/Self(.31)	God(.40), Unconscious/ Self(.35)
Leans Towards Some +	Unconscious/Me(.26)	
Low +	Life(.16), Unconscious(.13), Unknown(.10)	White(.16), Waking/Day (.11)
Very Low +	Consciousness(.09), Dream/Night(.05), God (.03), White(.01)	Death(.09), Black(.04), Black Race(.04), Unconscious(.02)

Table 4 (cont.) Clustering of Factor Loadings of the Fifteen Concepts on the Evaluative Dimension for Outer vs. and Inner-Oriented Respondents

Factor III (cont.)

Low -	White Race(-.13)	Unknown(-.16)
Very Low -	Satan(-.05)	Dream/Night(-.09), Satan (-.09)

<u>Factor IV</u>

High +	Satan(.70)	Black(.85), Satan(.68)
Some +	Black(.41)	
Low +	Unknown(.19), Unconscious/Self(.16), Consciousness(.12)	Death(.12), Waking/Day (.12)
Very Low +	Unconscious/Me(.009), White Race(.008)	Black Race(.09), Unconscious/Self(.001)
Mod. High -	God(-.55)	White(-.56)
Some -	White(-.39)	God(-.33)
Low -	Waking/Day(-.21), Black Race(-.17), Life(-.12)	Consciousness(-.19), Unconsciousness/Me (-.12), White Race(-.11)
Very Low -	Unconscious(-.03), Death (-.007), Dream/Night (-.0008)	Unknown(-.09), Dream/ Night(-.09), Unconscious(-.06), Life(-.01)

<u>Factor V</u>

High +	Life(.85)	Waking/Day(.70)
Mod. High +		Consciousness(.47)
Leans Towad Some +	Dream/Night(.28)	

Table 4. (cont.) Clustering of Factor Loadings of the Fifteen Concepts on the Evaluative Dimension for Outer vs. Inner-Oriented Ss.

Factor V (cont.)

Low +	Consciousness(.23), Black(.23), Waking/Day (.21), Unconscious(.17), Black Race(.16), Un-Known(.14), White Race (.14)	Black Race(.21), Life (.20), Dream/Night(.20), Satan(.11), Unconscious/ Me(.10)
Very Low +	God(.09), Unconscious/ Me(.09), Satan(.002)	Death(.08), White(.06), Unconscious(.02), Un-known(.01), Black(.009)
Low -	White(-.17)	Unconscious/Self(-.23), God(-.22)
Very Low -	Death(-.08), Uncon-scious/Self(-.04)	White Race(-.01)

respondents the priority focus was "The Nature of the Unconscious Portions of Me" (high +), while for the Inner-oriented respondents the priority focus was "The Nature of the Dreaming State (Night)" (high +). For Outer-oriented respondents, the race-linked colors and the race names did not load significantly on Factor I, though the colors ("black," low +; "white," low -) showed a bipolar tendency and "The Black Race" (low +) was weighted slightly higher than "The White Race" (low +) on this Factor. For Inner-oriented respondents, the race-linked colors and the race names also did not load significantly on Factor I, though "The Black Race" (low +) and the color "white" (very low +) were weighted higher and closer together than "The White Race" and the color "black." A reverse associative tendency for Inner-oriented respondents regarding race and color seemed to be present. Evaluatively, then, as "The Nature of the Unconscious" is thought about (evaluated) personally and generally, Outer-oriented respondents directly associated their evaluative thoughts (attributions) about "The Nature of" the Dreaming State and probably Death. Evaluatively, as "The Nature of the Dreaming State" is thought about (evaluated), Inner-oriented respondents directly associated their evaluative thoughts (attributions) about "The Nature of the Unconscious" personally and generally and probably their evaluative thoughts (attributions) about the Unknown.

On Factor II for Outer-oriented respondents, in an Evaluative context, a "white-Consciousness-White Race-Waking State-Life" association was linked to a bipolar "Unconscious-Dreaming State" association. For Inner-oriented respondents, Factor II indicated that in an Evaluative context, a "Death-Black Race-Unknown-Unconscious" association was directly linked to a "God-Life-Waking State" association. The priority focus, here, for Outer-oriented respondents on Factor II was the color "white" (high +). The priority focus for Inner-oriented respondents on Factor II was "The Nature of Death" (high +). For Outer-oriented respondents, the color "black" (low -) and "The Black Race" did not load significantly on Factor II, though both items loaded bipolarly along with "The Nature of the Dreaming State (Night)" and the religious concepts ("Satan," low -; "God," low -). For Inner-oriented respondents, the color "black" (low +) and "The White Race" (very low -) did not load significantly on Factor II, though the colors tended to load bipolarly and "The White Race" loaded bipolarly in accord with the color "white" (very low -). Evaluatively, then, as the color "white" is thought about (evaluated), Outer-oriented respondents directly associated the predicted links among "The Nature of" Consciousness, the White Race, the Waking State, and Life, and juxtaposed bipolarly their evaluative thoughts (attributions) about "The Nature of" the Unconscious in general and the Dreaming State. Evaluatively, as "The Nature of Death" is thought about (evaluated), Inner-oriented respondents directly link their evaluative thoughts (attributions) about the Black Race and the Unknown with their evaluative thoughts (attributions) about "The Nature of" God, Life, the Waking State, and probably the Unconscious in general and personal terms.

On Factor III for Outer-oriented respondents, in an Evaluative context, a "Death-black-Black Race-Unconscious" association was directly linked to "The Nature of the Waking State (Day)." For Inner-oriented respondents, Factor III indicated that in an Evaluation context, a "White Race-Consciousness-Life-God" association was directly linked to a personalized "Unconscious" in terms of "Me" and "the Self." The priority focus for Outer-oriented respondents here was "The

Nature of Death" (high +); the priority focus for Inner-oriented respondents was "The White Race" (high +). For Outer-oriented respondents, the color "white" (very low +) and "The White Race" (low -) did not load significantly on Factor III, but interestingly they tended to load bipolarly (in slightly different directions) to each other. For Inner-oriented respondents, the race-linked colors ("black," very low +; "white," low +) and "The Black Race" (very low +) did not load significantly on Factor III, though "white" was weighted slightly higher than "black" and "The Black Race." Evaluatively, then, as "The Nature of Death" is thought about (evaluated), Outer-oriented respondents directly linked their evaluative thoughts (attributions) about the color black and the Black Race with their evaluative thoughts (attributions) about "The Nature of the Waking State" and a personalized Unconscious. That is, as "The Nature of Death" is evaluated by Outer-oriented respondents, perhaps the Black Race, associated with the color black like Death, symbolizes the personalized Unconscious during the Waking State for these respondents. This is logically consistent with the general premise of the study. Evaluatively, as the self-reference group is thought about (evaluated), Inner-oriented respondents directly associate their evaluative thoughts (attributions) about "The Nature of" Consciousness, Life, God, and a personalized Unconscious.

On Factor IV for both Outer- and Inner-oriented respondents, in an Evaluative context, bipolar associations, respectively, between the race-linked colors ("white" and "black") and the religious concepts ("God" and "Satan") were clearly demonstrated, even though the priority focus for each group was different (i.e., a "black-Satan" association was linked bipolarly to a "white-God" association). For Outer-oriented respondents, the priority focus was "The Nature of Satan" (high +), while the priority focus for Inner-oriented respondents was the color "black" (high +). For Outer-oriented respondents, the race names did not load significantly on this Factor, though interestingly "The White Race" (very low +) and "The Black Race" (low -) loaded in the opposite associative manner with respect to the race-linked colors. For Inner-oriented respondents, the race names ("The Black Race," very low +; "The White Race," low -) did not load significantly on this Factor, but they did tend to load bipolarly in accord with the respective race-linked colors. So, in regard to the associative links on these Factors, overall the religious concepts loaded higher for Outer-oriented respondents, while the race-linked colors loaded higher for Inner-oriented respondents. Nevertheless, the predicted links between the religious concepts and the respective race-linked colors were clearly evident for both Outer- and Inner-oriented respondents.

On the final Factor, in an Evaluative context, for Outer-oriented respondents, the only significant loading was "The Nature of Life" (highest loading item, high +), with "The Nature of the Dreaming State (Night)" leaning toward some loading (+ direction). The race-linked colors ("black," low +; "white," low -) and the race names ("The Black Race," low +; "The White Race," low +) did not load significantly on this Factor, though the colors tended to load bipolarly and the race names did not. For Inner-oriented respondents, on Factor V, the final priority focus was "The Nature of the Waking State (Day)" (highest loading item, high +). The only other significant association on this Factor was to "The Nature of Consciousness" (moderately high +). The race names ("The Black Race," low +; "The White Race," very low -) and the race-linked colors ("black," very low +; "white," very low +) did not load significantly on this Factor, though the race names tended to be slightly bipolar and the race-linked colors did not. So, evaluatively, Outer-oriented respondents slightly associated their evaluative thoughts (attributions) about "The Nature of Life" with their evaluative thoughts (attributions) about "The Nature of the Dreaming State." For Inner-oriented respondents, evaluative thoughts (attributions) about daytime issues were clearly linked to evaluative thoughts (attributions) about "The Nature of Consciousness."

In general, then, the Outer vs Inner orientation did make a difference (sometimes a subtle difference) in how Ss linked the concepts together in terms of Fear and Evaluation on most of the Factors and, in most cases, in terms of which stimulus items emerged as a priority focus (validation for part of Hypothesis 1-b). While the overall clustering patterns in regard to Fear and Evaluation were much more complex than had been anticipated, some of the predicted links among the concepts did occur. That is, a number of independent associative patterns were found for Outer-oriented respondents and Inner-oriented respondents in regard to Fear and Evaluation. Despite this, the empirically-derived Factors were logically consistent with the general premises of the study. In fact, a "black-Black Race-Unconscious" association and a "white-White Race-Consciousness" association were clearly demonstrated, and Outer- and Inner-oriented respondents did deal with these associations somewhat differently in regard to Fear and Evaluation.

More specifically, both a "black-Black Race-Unconscious" association, and a "white-White Race-Consciousness" association were more pronounced for Outer-oriented respondents in an Evaluative context, as they focused, respectively, on the issue of "The Nature of Death" (Factor III) and the color "white" (Factor II). A few other concepts were also significantly associated here (i.e., "The Nature of the Waking State" for both associations; "The Nature of Life" and a bipolar "Unconscious-Dreaming State" link for the latter association). In the context of Fear, Outer-oriented respondents linked a "Death-Black Race-Dreaming State-black" association directly to a "God-White Race-Waking State" association, as they focused on the issue of "The Nature of Death" (Factor II). Comparatively, for Inner-oriented respondents, a "black-Black Race-Unconscious" association was actually more pronounced for them in the context of Fear, as they focused on "The Unknown" (Factor II). "The Nature of" the Dreaming State and Satan were also significantly linked here, but interestingly not the concept of "The Nature of Death."

In an Evaluative context, Inner-oriented respondents linked a "Death-Black Race-Unknown-Unconscious" association directly to a "God-Life-Waking State" association, as they focused on the issue of "The Nature of Death" (Factor II). There was no significant link here to the color "black" by Inner-oriented respondents. Further, in both Fear (Factor III) and Evaluative (Factor III) contexts, a "White Race-Consciousness" association was maintained by Inner-oriented respondents and was linked significantly to a few other concepts (i.e., "The Nature of Life," "The Nature of God," and a "personalized Unconscious" in the Evaluative context; bipolarly to "The Nature of the Dreaming State" in the context of Fear), but this association was not significantly linked to the color "white" by Inner-oriented respondents.

So, while the overall clustering patterns did not occur "exactly" as had been predicted for Outer-oriented respondents and Inner-oriented respondents, the associative patterns that were found tended to validate Hypothesis 1 logically and to demonstrate the differential impact of an Outer vs Inner orientation on associative thought processes (or patterns of attributions). Further, the findings seemed to support the idea that, for some Caucasians, the Black Race in the American culture may represent the Unconscious Self symbolically in "meaning space" (via associative links), while the White Race may represent the Conscious Self and that

Outer-oriented respondents tend to associatively use "both" the race-linked colors more so than Inner-oriented respondents in this regard.

The overtones of religion, particularly the implication that people fear (or have fearful attributions, probably due to the projection of power, about) "The Nature of God," was also very much in evidence in the results of the factor analyses. The findings seemed to validate a link among color, race, and ideas about God and Satan, particularly the link between the religious concepts and the race-inked colors (i.e., for Outer-oriented respondents, Factors I, II, IV, V in the context of Fear and Factor IV in the Evaluative context; for Inner-oriented respondents, Factors II and V in the context of Fear and Factors II, III, and IV in the Evaluative context). Associatively, the concept of God tended to emerge more often for Outer-oriented respondents than for Inner-oriented respondents. This is consistent with another finding that Outer-oriented respondents tended to go to church more often than Inner-oriented respondents.

There was also some support for the idea that associations (associative attributions) about "The Nature of" the Dreaming State and the Waking State are linked to asociations (associative attributions) about race and "The Nature of" Consciousness and the Unconscious. The findings here, however, suggest a more complex relationship, which depended, in part, on the person's Outer or Inner orientation, the priority focus, and the context in which the concepts were being considered. For example, while Outer-oriented respondents, evaluatively, linked both "The Nature of the Waking State" and "The Nature of the Dreaming State" in "meaning space" to a "white-White Race-Consciousness" association (Factor II) and linked "The Nature of the Waking State" only to a "black-Black Race-Unconscious" association (Factor III), they directly linked, in the context of Fear, a "black-Black Race-Dreaming State" association to a "White Race-Waking State" association. For Inner-oriented respondents, "The Nature of the Dreaming State" was linked directly to a "black-Black Race-Unconscious" association in the context of Fear (Factor II) and "The Nature of the Waking State" was linked directly to a "Death-Black Race-Unknown-Unconscious" association. For both groups, however, an "Unconscious-Dreaming State" association and a "Consciousness-Waking State" association were clearly evident, but emerged differentially for each group depending on the context.

A final observation is that Outer- and Inner-oriented respondents dealt with a "Death-Black Race-Unconscious" association somewhat differently. That is, while evaluatively both Outer- and Inner-oriented respondents linked "The Black Race" directly to the "The Nature of the Unconscious" as each group focused on the issue of "The Nature of Death" (Factors III and II, respectively), Outer-oriented respondents, in the context of Fear, significantly maintained a "Death-Black Race" association, but not a "Black Race-Unconscious" association (Factor II). This "Death-Black Race" association was supported or reinforced by its link to the color "black," and the self-reference group also surfaced here. On the other hand, Inner-oriented respondents, in the context of Fear, significantly maintained the "Black Race-Unconscious" association, but not the "Death-Black Race" association, as they focused on "The Unknown" (Factor II). These findings have implications for how Outer- and Inner-oriented respondents may differentially link the Black Race to their perceptions of "The Nature of Death" as the annihilation of Consciousness.

Overall, the above findings regarding the associative links in "meaning space" among the various concepts for Outer- and Inner-oriented respondents appear to be reflecting some deeply engrained cultural Fears (or Fear-related cultural attributions) and Evaluative orientations to which Caucasian individuals are exposed in the "cultural meaning space" in developing a sense of Self, not-Self, and the world. That is, growing up Caucasian or White in the United States apparently reinforces, encourages, and/or supports many of these conceptual links in terms of Fears (or Fearful attributions) and Evaluative judgments, with the Outer vs Inner orientations serving, at times, to influence the person's priority focus, modify the salience of certain concepts, or mask the general associative links in "meaning space" among the concepts. It can be theorized that the priority foci for the various Factors constitute "core concepts" that may emerge and interact in an interracial context, along with their "associative thought patterns" (or patterns of associative attributions) to target the Black Race for anti-black prejudice. Even those Caucasians with a more Inner orientation, then, may get influenced by a culturally conditioned, Extraceptive bias in thinking about (or making attributions about) the meanings of Color, Race, Religion, Day and Night, Consciousness and the Unconscious, Life and Death, and the Unknown in American culture.

The relationship between the Outer vs Inner orientations and the overall salience of the various stimulus concepts used in this study is reflected in a series of findings outlined below. These findings help to assess the importance of the various Factors to each group in terms of the variance accounted for by the Factor and in terms of the significant stimulus items on the Factors. They also help to explain further how Outer- and Inner-oriented respondents differentially dealt with the various concepts.

Table 5 provides a summary of the relative importance of the Factors that emerged on the Fear and Evaluative dimensions of the SD for Outer-oriented respondents and Inner-oriented respondents. As can be seen, while the first Factor was the most important in terms of the variance accounted for, the subsequent and secondary Factors were also relatively important. Principal factoring analysis was done in all cases. The Factors that were found in this study indicated intricate direct, and sometimes bipolar, relationships among the various stimulus items. That is, while some of the Factors reflected some of the predicted links, the nature of the relationships among the stimulus items depended on which stimulus item loaded highest on a particular Factor, which dimension or context was being considered (i.e., Fear or Evaluative), and the respondents' Outer or Inner orientation. When the importance (i.e., variance accounted for) of the various Factors for Outer-oriented respondents and Inner-oriented respondents are examined more closely and compared in terms of what stimulus items loaded significantly on the Factors, it is possible to evaluate the relative saliency of the various stimulus items (how often it showed up) in the context of a given dimension. Further, it is possible to get a sense of what role an Outer vs Inner orientation plays in regard to this saliency.

In terms of the race-linked colors, the color "black," in the context of Fear, loaded significantly on Factors II and III (accounting for 31.7% of the variance) for Outer-oriented respondents, while the color "white" loaded significantly on Factor V (accounting for 8.2% of the variance). For Inner-oriented respondents, in the context of Fear, the color "black" loaded significantly on Factors II and IV (accounting for 30.3% of the variance), while the color "white" loaded significantly on Factor IV (accounting for 12.1% of the variance). The net effect of the Outer and Inner orientations, then, in regard to the race-linked colors was to increase the salience of the color "black" in the context of Fear. That is, it would appear that if a person's orientation becomes operative in the context of Fear, the sensitivity to the color "black" may become heightened as Ss look outwardly and think about (make

Table 5. Summary of the Relative Importance (i.e., Variance Accounted For) of the Various Factors that were Found on the Fear and Evaluative Dimensions for Outer-Oriented Respondents and Inner-Oriented Respondents

I. Relative Importance of the Factors that were Found in Regard to the Fear Dimension for the Fifteen Concepts

	Outer-Oriented Ss				Inner-Oriented Ss		
Factor	Eigen-Value	% of Var.	Cum. %	Factor	Eigen-Value	% of Var.	Cum. %
I	3.55	48.5	48.5	I	3.16	43.2	43.2
II	1.32	18.0	66.5	II	1.33	18.2	61.5
III	1.00	13.7	80.1	III	1.29	17.6	79.0
IV	.85	11.6	91.8	IV	.89	12.1	91.1
V	.60	8.2	100.0	V	.65	8.9	100.0

II. Relative Importance of the Factors that were Found in Regard to the Evaluative Dimension for the Fifteen Concepts

	Outer-Oriented Ss				Inner-Oriented Ss		
Factor	Eigen-Value	% of Var.	Cum. %	Factor	Eigen-Value	% of Var.	Cum. %
I	3.43	43.5	43.5	I	3.73	42.7	42.7
II	2.05	25.9	69.4	II	1.94	22.2	64.9
III	.97	12.3	81.7	III	1.29	14.7	79.6
IV	.75	9.5	91.2	IV	1.02	11.7	91.3
V	.69	8.8	100.0	V	.79	8.7	100.0

attributions about) "The Nature of" Death and Satan or look inwardly and think about (make attributions about) the Unknown and "The Nature of Life." Despite the increased salience for the color "black," Outer-oriented respondents may have as a priority focus the color "white" in the context of Fear when linked to "The Nature of God" and "The Unknown" (Factor V).

In terms of the race names, Outer-oriented respondents, in the context of Fear, directly linked both race names in a significant way on Factor II. This Factor accounted for 18% of the overall variance. For Inner-oriented respondents, in the context of Fear, "The Black Race" loaded significantly on Factor II (accounting for 18.2% of the variance) and "The White Race" loaded significantly on Factor III (accounting for 17.6% of the variance). It would appear, then, that while the Inner-oriented Caucasian respondents dealt with the saliency of the race names independently in the context of Fear, the Outer-oriented respondents were prone to directly link them in a significant way when Fear (i.e., more specifically, Fear of "The Nature of Death") is an issue. Overall, however, the degree of salience for the race names did not appear to be affected by a person's orientation.

In terms of the Unconscious and Consciousness concepts, the findings are clear that "The Nature of the Unconscious" was a very salient consideration for these Caucasians Ss in the context of Fear. For Outer-oriented respondents, in the context of Fear, at least one of the Unconscious stimulus items was significantly reflected on Factors I and IV (accounting for 60.1% of the variance), while "The Nature of Consciousness" loaded significantly on Factors I and III (accounting for 62.2% of the variance). For Inner-oriented respondents, in the context of Fear, at least one of the Unconscious stimulus items was significantly reflected on Factors I and II (accounting for 61.4% of the variance), while "The Nature of Consciousness" loaded significantly on Factor III (accounting for 17.6% of the variance). By and large, the more personalized Unconscious stimulus items (i.e., "The Nature of the Unconscious Portions of Me" and "The Nature of the Unconscious Portions of the Self"), which appeared to be links between a person's Outer and Inner life experiences, were more salient on the various Factors than "The Nature of the Unconscious" in general. In the context of Fear, then, "The Nature of the Unconscious" remained relatively salient, irrespective of a person's orientation (actually, the Outer-Inner orientations decreased the salience slightly). Further, an Outer orientation substantially increased the salience of "The Nature of Consciousness," while an Inner orientation did not.

In the context of Fear, "The Nature of the Waking State (Day)" loaded significantly on Factors I and II (accounting for 66.5% of the variance) for Outer-oriented respondents, while "The Nature of the Dreaming State (Night)" loaded significantly on Factors II and IV (accounting for 29.6% of the variance). For Inner-oriented respondents, in the context of Fear, "The Nature of the Waking State (Day)" loaded significantly on Factor I (accounting for 43.2% of the variance), while "The Nature of the Dreaming State (Night)" loaded significantly on Factors I, II and III (accounting for 79.0% of the variance). Generally, then, in the context of Fear, while both stimulus items tended to be somewhat salient, "The Nature of the Dreaming State (Night)" tended to be slightly more salient than "The Nature of the

Waking State (Day)." It would appear, however, that an Outer orientation tended to increase the salience of "The Nature of the Waking State (Day)" and to decrease the salience of "The Nature of the Dreaming State (Night)." An Inner orientation, on the other hand, apparently further increased the salience of "The Nature of the Dreaming State (Night)."

In the context of Fear, "The Nature of Life" loaded significantly on Factors III and IV (accounting for 25.3% of the variance) for Outer-oriented respondents, while "The Nature of Death" loaded significantly on Factor II (accounting for 18.0% of the variance). For Inner-oriented respondents, in the context of Fear, "The Nature of Life" loaded significantly on Factors IV and V (accounting for 21.0% of the variance), while "The Nature of Death" loaded significantly on Factors I and IV (accounting for 55.3% of the variance). It would appear, however, that for most of these Caucasians Ss, in the context of Fear, "The Nature of" Life and Death tended to be latent considerations. An Outer orientation may not impact that much on the salience for "The Nature of Life," but an Inner orientation tended to substantially increase the salience for "The Nature of Death." Despite this, when Fear becomes operative, Outer-oriented respondents, ironically, may have as a priority focus concerns about "The Nature of Death" (Factor II), while Inner-oriented respondents may have as a priority focus concerns about "The Nature of Life" (Factors IV and V).

In terms of the religious concepts, the concept of God, in the context of Fear, loaded significantly on Factors I, II, IV and V (accounting for 86.3% of the variance) for Outer-oriented respondents, while the concept of Satan loaded significantly on Factor III (accounting for 13.7% of the variance). For Inner-oriented respondents, in the context of Fear, the concept of God loaded significantly on Factor V (accounting for 8.9% of the variance), while the concept of Satan loaded significantly on Factor II (accounting for 18.2% of the variance). An Outer orientation apparently tended to substantially increase the salience for the concept of God, while an Inner orientation seemed to decrease the salience (that is, the concept of God may tend to recede further). No significant differences seemed to occur as a result of a person's Outer vs Inner orientation for the concept of Satan. Outer-oriented respondents may have the concept of Satan, however, as a priority focus in the context of Fear (Factor III).

The concept of "The Unknown," in the Fear context, loaded significantly on Factors I, III and V (accounting for 70.4% of the variance) for Outer-oriented respondents. For Inner-oriented respondents, in the context of Fear, "The Unknown" loaded significantly on Factor II (accounting for 18.2% of the variance). In general, then, the concept of "The Unknown" had some salience for most of the Caucasians Ss, in the context of Fear. An Outer orientation tended to substantially increase the salience for "The Unknown," while an Inner orientation seemed to decrease the saliency. Despite this, as the context of Fear becomes operative, Inner-oriented respondents may tend to have as a priority focus "The Unknown" (Factor II), while Outer-oriented respondents may tend to use the concept of "The Unknown" associatively to support or reinforce other priority foci (e.g., Factor I, the Unconscious in terms of "me" and "the self"; Factor III, "The Nature of Satan"; Factor V, the color "white" in association with the concept of God).

In terms of the race-linked colors, evaluatively, the color "black" loaded significantly on Factor IV (accounting for 21.8% of the variance) for Outer-oriented respondents, while the color "white" loaded significantly on Factors II and IV (accounting for 35.4% of the variance). For Inner-oriented respondents, evaluatively, both the race-linked colors loaded significantly on Factors III and IV (accounting for 11.7% of the variance). While the saliency for both race-linked colors appeared not to be too high in the Evaluative context, the color "white" tended to be slightly more salient in the Evaluative context than the color "black" for Outer-oriented respondents. In fact, Outer-oriented respondents had as a priority focus the color "white" (Factor II), while Inner-oriented respondents had as a priority focus the color "black" (Factor IV) in the Evaluative context.

In terms of the race names, evaluatively, "The Black Race" loaded significantly on Factor III (accounting for 12.3% of the variance) for Outer-oriented respondents and "The White Race" loaded significantly on Factor II (accounting for 25.9% of the variance). For Inner-oriented respondents, evaluatively, "The Black Race" loaded significantly on Factor II (accounting for 22.2% of the variance) and "The White Race" loaded significantly on Factor III (accounting for 14.7% of the variance). For Outer-oriented respondents, the self-reference group ("The White Race") was slightly more salient, evaluatively, than "The Black Race"; the reverse tended to be the case for Inner-oriented respondents, despite the fact that these respondents had as a priority focus the self-reference group (Factor III).

In terms of the Unconscious, evaluatively, again the findings are clear that "The Nature of the Unconscious" was a very salient consideration. For Outer-oriented respondents, evaluatively, at least one of the Unconscious items loaded significantly on Factors I, II and III (accounting for 81.7% of the variance), while "The Nature of Consciousness" loaded significantly on Factor II (accounting for 25.9% of the variance). For Inner-oriented respondents, evaluatively, at least one of the Unconscious items was significantly reflected on Factors I, II and III (accounting for 79.6% of the variance), while "The Nature of Consciousness" loaded significantly on Factors III and V (accounting for 23.4% of the variance). Evaluatively, then, it would appear that "The Nature of the Unconscious" is a substantially more salient consideration than "The Nature of Consciousness," irrespective of a person's Outer or Inner orientation.

Evaluatively, "The Nature of the Waking State (Day)" loaded significantly on Factors II and III (accounting for 38.2% of the variance) for Outer-oriented respondents, while "The Nature of the Dreaming State (Night)" loaded significantly on Factors I, II and V (accounting for 78.2% of the variance). For Inner-oriented respondents, evaluatively, "The Nature of the Waking State (Day)" loaded significantly on Factors II and V (accounting for 30.9% of the variance), while "The Nature of the Dreaming State (Night)" loaded significantly on Factor I (accounting for 42.7% of the variance). Interestingly, an Outer orientation apparently increased the saliency of "The Nature of the Dreaming State (Night)" in the Evaluative context, but this saliency operated associatively in a reinforcing or supportive way. An Inner orientation, however, had as priority foci both items in the Evaluative context, with "The Nature of the Dreaming State (Night)" being a higher (i.e., more important consideration in terms of variance accounted for) priority focus (Factor I) than "The Nature of the Waking State (Day)" (Factor V). Overall, "The Nature of the Dreaming State (Night)" appeared to be a bit more salient than "The Nature of the Waking State (Day)."

Evaluatively, "The Nature of Life" loaded significantly on Factors II and V (accounting for 34.7% of the variance) for Outer-oriented respondents, while "The Nature of Death" loaded significantly on Factors I and III (accounting for 55.8% of the variance). For Inner-oriented respondents, evaluatively, "The Nature of Life" loaded significantly on Factors II and III (accounting for 36.9% of the variance), while "The Nature of Death" loaded significantly on Factor II (accounting for 22.2% of the variance). Generally, then, in the Evaluative context, "The Nature of Life" appeared to be more salient for most of the Caucasian Ss than "The Nature of Death." When a person's orientation, however, is taken into account, an Outer orientation tended to increase the salience of "The Nature of Death." Both orientations, however, had as a priority focus "The Nature of Death" in the Evaluative context.

In terms of the religious concepts, evaluatively, both "The Nature of God" and "The Nature of Satan" loaded significantly on Factor IV (accounting for 9.5% of the variance) for Outer-oriented respondents. For Inner-oriented respondents, evaluatively, "The Nature of God" loaded significantly on Factors II, III and IV (accounting for 48.6% of the variance) and "The Nature of Satan" loaded significantly on Factor IV (accounting for 11.7% of the variance). Basically, then, most of the Caucasian Ss tended to link the religious concepts bipolarly and the salience of these concepts appeared to be latent considerations in the Evaluative context. An Inner orientation, however, may increase the salience of "The Nature of God" in the Evaluative context, but this saliency operates associatively in a reinforcing or supportive way. An Outer orientation, on the other hand, has as a priority focus "The Nature of Satan" in the Evaluative context.

For Outer-oriented respondents, evaluatively, the concept of "The Unknown" did not load significantly on any Factors. For Inner-oriented respondents, evaluatively, "The Unknown" was reflected significantly on Factors I and II (accounting for 64.9% of the variance). In general, then, the concept of "The Unknown" in the Evaluative context may be a latent consideration for most of the Caucasian Ss. An Inner orientation, however, apparently increased the salience of "The Unknown," while an Outer orientation apparently led to an avoidance of "The Unknown" altogether in the Evaluative context.

In terms of Fear and Evaluation, then, the Outer vs Inner orientations may have some differential impact on the salience of some concepts as these two groups give meaning to their worlds. In some cases, whether or not the salience of a concept was increased, decreased, or remained relatively unchanged depended on the context (i.e., Fear or Evaluative) in which the concept was being considered. It also seemed that the salience of certain concepts may increase as a result of the person's orientation, but this increased salience was often due to the concept being significantly associated as a supportive or reinforcing concept to some other priority concept. Also, a concept could be used as a priority focus without necessarily being overall salient.

Affective Meanings of Proposed Race-linked Concepts or Constructs

To further understand the meaning of the various Factors that were found, the affective meanings for each concept or construct were examined for Outer-oriented respondents and Inner-oriented respondents. Hypothesis 1-a predicted that the stimulus items "black," "The Black Race," "The Nature of the Unconscious," "The Nature of the Dreaming State (Night)," "The Nature of Death," "The Nature of Satan," and "The Unknown" would have similar affective meanings and that the stimulus items "white," "The White Race," "The Nature of Consciousness," "The Nature of the Waking State (Day)," "The Nature of Life," and "The Nature of God" would have similar affective meanings. Hypothesis 1-a further predicted that there would be a polarizing effect in regard to the affective meanings for these respective subsets of concepts and that the former subset of concepts would be evaluated more negatively, while the latter subset of concepts would be evaluated more positively. Hypothesis 1-b predicted that overall Outer- and Inner-oriented respondents would deal with (rate on a SD) the various concepts in somewhat different ways.

Overall mean scores for each concept in relation to a particular dimension and mean scores for each concept in relation to each of the bipolar adjectives (i.e., specific quality or affective meaning) on a particular dimension were determined. Tests of significance (t-tests) were also used to examine significant differences between Outer- and Inner-oriented respondents in terms of their overall response to a concept on a particular dimension and in terms of their specific-quality or affective meaning response to a concept. For interpretive purposes, mean scores of 1 to 3 were interpreted as "passive," "weak," "relaxed," "nonfrightening" (Low Fear qualities or affective meanings on the Fear dimension), "dark," "bad," "primitive," "dirty," "profane" (Negative qualities or affective meanings on the Evaluative dimension), "mysterious," "strange," "chaotic" (Low Understandability qualities or affective meanings on the Understandability dimension), and "powerless" and "weak" (Low Potency on the Potency dimension); means scores of 3.01 to 3.5 and 4.5 to 4.99 were interpreted as a "Tendency Toward" the respective end of the scale; mean scores greater than 3.5 but less than 4.5 were interpreted as "Neutral or Ambivalent" responses; and mean scores of 5 to 7 were interpreted as "active," "strong," "tense," "frightening" (High Fear qualities or affective meanings on the Fear dimension), "bright," "good," "civilized," "clean," "sacred" (Positive qualities or affective meanings on the Evaluative dimension) and "powerful" and "strong" (High Potency on the Potency dimension). It should be noted that an overall Neutral or Ambivalent response might actually mean that qualities or affective meanings from both sides of a dimension were present and simply balanced or neutralized the overall response (e.g., a concept or construct may be "dark" and "good," evaluatively), or that one or two qualities or affective meanings on a given dimension were present but not others and this balanced or neutralized the overall response. While not contained in Hypothesis 1, the Understandability dimension and Potency dimension were included to provide a fuller picture of what the concepts or constructs meant to Ss .

Overall, when Outer-oriented respondents and Inner-oriented respondents were compared to each other in terms of their overall response to a concept or construct on a given dimension (i.e., Fear, Evaluative, etc.) and in terms of their specific response in regard to a given quality or affective meaning (i.e., dark-bright) on a particular dimension (e.g., Evaluative) for a concept (e.g., black), a number of significant differences were found between the two groups. Table 6 gives a profile of all the significant and near significant findings, while Table 7 provides a comparison of the mean scores for each concept in relation to the 13 bipolar adjectives (specific qualities or affective meanings for each concept on the dimensions).

As can be seen in Table 6, then, the SD ratings by Outer-oriented respondents indicated Lower Understandabilty for the color "black" than the SD ratings by Inner-oriented respondents. In terms of specific qualities or affective meanings, the SD ratings by Outer-oriented respondents indicated that the color "black" was significantly "stranger," significantly "chaotic" (as opposed to a "Neutral" rating by Inner-oriented respondents in regard to the chaotic-organized quality), and somewhat more "bad," when compared to the SD ratings by Inner-

Table 6. *Test Of Significant Differences Between Outer-oriented Respondents and Inner-oriented Respondents in terms of their Respective Overall Connotative Responses to a Concept on a Given Dimension and in terms of their Specific Response to a Given Affective Meaning for a Concept on a Particular Dimension*

I. **Significant Differences in terms of Overall Connotative Responses to a Concept on a Given Dimension**

VARIABLES (DIMENSIONS)	n	M	SD	SE	F	p (two-tail)*	Pooled Variance Estimate			Separate Variance Estimate		
							t	df	p	t	df	p
Black(Understandability Dimension)												
Outer-oriented	60	2.50	1.16	.15	1.04	.88	-1.94	118	.055	-1.94	117.96	.055
Inner-oriented	60	2.91	1.14	.15								
White(Potency Dimension)												
Outer-oriented	60	5.03	1.77	.23	1.14	.61	2.66	118	.009	2.66	117.49	.009
Inner-oriented	60	4.13	1.90	.25								
Unconscious/Self (Fear Dimension)												
Outer-oriented	60	4.44	1.01	.13	1.47	.14	-2.16	118	.03	-2.16	113.85	.03
Inner-oriented	60	4.80	.83	.11								
Unconscious/Self (Potency Dimension)												
Outer-oriented	60	4.90	1.30	.17	1.59	.078	-2.48	118	.015	-2.48	112.20	.015
Inner-oriented	60	5.43	1.04	.13								

*In the Table, if the probability of F is greater than the .05 or .01 level of significance, H_0 is accepted; t based on the pooled variance estimate should be used as the appropriate test. If the probability for F is less than or equal to the .05 or .10 level of significance, H_0 is rejected; t based on the separate variance estimate should be used as the appropriate test.

Cont. Table 6. Differences Between Outer- and Inner-Oriented Respondents in Overall Connotative Responses to the Concepts

VARIABLES (DIMENSIONS)	n	M	SD	SE	F	p (two-tail)	Pooled Variance Estimate			Separate Variance Estimate		
							t	df	p	t	df	p
Consciousness(Evaluative Dimension)												
Outer-oriented	60	5.42	.95	.12	1.29	.32	2.37	118	.02	2.37	116.09	.02
Inner-oriented	60	4.98	1.08	.14								
Consciousness(Potency Dimension)												
Outer-oriented	60	5.58	1.01	.13	1.28	.35	2.07	118	.04	2.07	116.27	.04
Inner-oriented	60	5.18	1.15	.15								
White Race(Evaluative Dimension)												
Outer-oriented	60	5.06	1.06	.14	1.30	.31	3.09	118	.003	3.09	116.01	.003
Inner-oriented	60	4.50	.93	.12								
White Race(Understandability Dimension)												
Outer-oriented	60	5.19	1.19	.15	1.10	.72	1.70	118	.09	1.70	117.70	.09
Inner-oriented	60	4.83	1.14	.15								
Life(Evaluative Dimension)												
Outer-oriented	60	5.29	.88	.11	1.12	.67	1.79	118	.076	1.79	117.60	.076
Inner-oriented	60	5.01	.83	.11								
Life(Understandability Dimension)												
Outer-oriented	60	4.05	1.42	.18	2.05	.007	3.94	118	.000	3.94	105.57	.001
Inner-oriented	60	3.17	.99	.13								

Cont. Table 6. **Differences Between Outer- and Inner-oriented Respondents in Overall Connotative Responses to the Concepts**

VARIABLES (DIMENSIONS)	n	M	SD	SE	F	p (two-tail)	Pooled Variance Estimate			Separate Variance Estimate		
							t	df	p	t	df	p
Life(Potency Dimension)												
Outer-oriented	60	5.78	.77	.10	1.65	.056	3.72	118	.000	3.72	111.25	.001
Inner-oriented	60	5.18	.99	.13								
Death(Evaluative Dimension)												
Outer-oriented	60	4.01	1.16	.15	1.26	.37	-2.37	118	.019	-2.37	116.42	.019
Inner-oriented	60	4.55	1.31	.17								
Waking State/Day (Understandability Dimension)												
Outer-oriented	60	5.38	.95	.12	1.71	.04	3.20	118	.002	3.20	110.48	.002
Inner-oriented	60	4.73	1.24	.16								
Unknown (Evaluative Dimension)												
Outer-oriented	60	3.63	.85	.11	1.82	.02	-1.89	118	.06	-1.89	108.80	.06
Inner-oriented	60	3.97	1.14	.15								
Satan(Understand-ability Dimension)												
Outer-oriented	60	2.17	1.30	.17	1.14	.62	-2.11	118	.037	-2.11	117.50	.037
Inner-oriented	60	2.68	1.38	.18								
God(Evaluative Dimension)												
Outer-oriented	60	6.46	.71	.09	2.08	.006	3.92	118	.000	3.92	105.13	.001
Inner-oriented	60	5.83	1.03	.13								

Cont. Table 6. Differences Between Outer- and Inner-oriented Respondents in Overall Connotative and Specific Affective Meaning Responses to the Concepts

VARIABLES (DIMENSIONS)	n	M	SD	SE	F	p (two-tail)	Pooled Variance Estimate			Separate Variance Estimate		
							t	df	p	t	df	p
God(Potency Dimension)												
Outer-oriented	60	6.73	.56	.07	6.32	.001	2.71	118	.008	2.71	77.22	.008
Inner-oriented	60	6.20	1.40	.18								

II.   Significant Differences in terms of Specific Responses to a Given Affective Meaning (i.e., Bipolar Adjectives) on a Particular Dimension

VARIABLES (Specific Affective Meanings) (DIMENSIONS)	n	M	SD	SE	F	p (two-tail)	Pooled Variance Estimate			Separate Variance Estimate		
							t	df	p	t	df	p
Black(bad-good) (Evaluative Dimension)												
Outer-oriented	60	2.47	1.41	.18	1.28	.34	-2.37	118	.02	-2.37	116.20	.02
Inner-oriented	60	3.12	1.60	.21								
Black(strange-familiar) (Understandability Dimension)												
Outer-oriented	60	2.67	1.48	.19	1.34	.26	-1.82	118	.07	-1.82	115.50	.07
Inner-oriented	60	3.20	1.72	.22								
Black(chaotic-organized) (Understandability Dimension)												
Outer-oriented	60	2.97	1.75	.23	1.10	.72	-2.35	118	.02	-2.35	117.70	.02
Inner-oriented	60	3.73	1.83	.24								

Cont. Table 6.   Differences Between Outer- and Inner-oriented Respondents in Specific Affective Meaning Responses to the Concepts

VARIABLES (Specific Affective Meanings) (DIMENSIONS)	n	M	SD	SE	F	p (two-tail)	Pooled Variance Estimate			Separate Variance Estimate		
							t	df	p	t	df	p
White(passive-active) (Fear Dimension)												
Outer-oriented	60	4.00	2.28	.29	1.12	.65	1.77	118	.079	1.77	117.60	.079
Inner-oriented	60	3.28	2.15	.28								
White(weak-strong) (Fear Dimension)												
Outer-oriented	60	4.93	1.94	.25	1.23	.42	2.23	118	.028	2.23	116.70	.028
Inner-oriented	60	4.10	2.15	.28								
White(profane-sacred) (Evaluative Dimension)												
Outer-oriented	60	5.63	1.66	.21	1.58	.08	-1.65	118	.10	-1.65	112.30	.10
Inner-oriented	60	6.08	1.32	.17								
White(powerless-powerful) (Potency Dimension)												
Outer-oriented	60	5.12	1.93	.25	1.05	.86	2.66	118	.009	2.66	117.90	.009
Inner-oriented	60	4.17	1.98	.26								
Unconscious(relaxed-tense) (Fear Dimension)												
Outer-oriented	60	4.17	1.67	.22	1.01	.96	-2.03	118	.045	-2.03	117.99	.045
Inner-oriented	60	4.78	1.66	.21								

Cont. Table 6. Differences Between Outer- and Inner-Oriented Respondents in Specific Affective Meaning Responses to the Concepts

VARIABLES (Specific Affective Meanings) (DIMENSIONS)	n	M	SD	SE	F	p (two-tail)	Pooled Variance Estimate			Separate Variance Estimate		
							t	df	p	t	df	p
Unconscious/Self (passive-active) (Fear Dimension)												
Outer-oriented	60	4.52	1.69	.22	1.26	.38	-1.77	118	.08	-1.77	116.40	.08
Inner-oriented	60	5.03	1.51	.20								
Unconscious/Self (weak-strong) (Fear Dimension)												
Outer-oriented	60	4.98	1.31	.17	1.28	.35	-2.07	118	.04	-2.07	116.40	.04
Inner-oriented	60	5.45	1.16	.15								
Unconscious/Self (powerless-powerful) (Potency Dimension)												
Outer-oriented	60	4.82	1.59	.21	1.45	.16	-2.25	118	.026	-2.25	114.10	.026
Inner-oriented	60	5.42	1.32	.17								
Unconscious/Me(primitive-civilized) (Understandability Dimension)												
Outer-oriented	60	4.05	1.67	.22	1.01	.96	1.63	118	.105	1.63	118	.105
Inner-oriented	60	3.55	1.68	.22								
Unconscious/Me (chaotic-organized) (Understandability Dimension)												
Outer-oriented	60	3.97	1.67	.22	1.20	.49	2.52	118	.01	2.52	117	.01
Inner-oriented	60	3.23	1.52	.20								

Cont. Table 6. Differences Between Outer- and Inner-oriented Respondents in Specific Affective Meaning Responses to the Concepts

VARIABLES (Specific Affective Meanings) (DIMENSIONS)	n	M	SD	SE	F	p (two tail)	Pooled Variance Estimate			Separated Variance Estimate		
							t	df	p	t	df	p
Consciousness(weak-strong) (Fear Dimension)												
Outer-oriented	60	5.60	1.14	.15	1.38	.22	1.76	118	.08	1.76	115.04	.08
Inner-oriented	60	5.20	1.34	.17								
Consciousness(relaxed-tense) (Fear Dimension)												
Outer-oriented	60	4.03	1.61	.21	1.03	.90	-1.69	118	.09	-1.69	117.97	.09
Inner-oriented	60	4.53	1.63	.21								
Consciousness(chaotic-organized) (Understandability Dimension)												
Outer-oriented	60	5.32	1.11	.14	2.05	.007	2.59	118	.01	2.59	105.60	.01
Inner-oriented	60	4.67	1.59	.21								
Consciousness(mysterious-understandable) (Understandability Dimension)												
Outer-oriented	60	5.42	1.39	.18	1.44	.17	1.66	118	.099	1.66	114.30	.099
Inner-oriented	60	4.95	1.67	.22								
Consciousness(powerless-powerful) (Potency Dimension)												
Outer-oriented	60	5.57	1.18	.15	1.33	.28	1.79	118	.076	1.79	117.70	.076
Inner-oriented	60	5.15	1.36	.18								

Cont. Table 6. **Differences Between Outer- and Inner-oriented Respondents in Specific Affective Meaning Responses to the Concepts**

VARIABLES (Specific Affective Meanings) (DIMENSIONS)	n	M	SD	SE	F	p(two-tail)	Pooled Variance Estimate			Separated Variance Estimate		
							t	df	p	t	df	p
Black Race(profane-sacred) (Evaluative Dimension)												
Outer-oriented	60	4.03	1.37	.18	1.43	.17	-1.81	118	.07	-1.81	114.40	.07
Inner-oriented	60	4.45	1.14	.15								
Black Race(bad-good) (Evaluative Dimension)												
Outer-oriented	60	4.25	1.30	.17	1.15	.58	-1.68	118	.096	-1.68	117.40	.096
Inner-oriented	60	4.63	1.21	.16								
White Race(dirty-clean) (Evaluative Dimension)												
Outer-oriented	60	5.07	1.23	.16	1.23	.43	1.96	118	.05	1.96	116.80	.05
Inner-oriented	60	4.60	1.37	.18								
White Race(profane-sacred) (Evaluative Dimension)												
Outer-oriented	60	4.53	1.23	.16	1.14	.61	2.15	118	.03	2.15	117.50	.03
Inner-oriented	60	4.07	1.15	.15								
White Race(bad-good) (Evaluative Dimension)												
Outer-oriented	60	5.05	1.32	.17	1.47	.14	3.09	118	.002	3.09	113.90	.002
Inner-oriented	60	4.37	1.09	.14								
White Race(dark-bright) (Evaluative Dimension)												
Outer-oriented	60	5.22	1.20	.15	1.10	.70	3.13	118	.002	3.13	117.70	.002
Inner-oriented	60	4.52	1.26	.16								

Cont. Table 6. Differences Between Outer- and Inner-oriented Respondents in Specific Affective Meaning Responses to the Concepts

VARIABLES (Specific Affective Meanings) (DIMENSIONS)	n	M	SD	SE	F	p (two-tail)	Pooled Variance Estimate			Separate Variance Estimate		
							t	df	p	t	df	p
White Race(chaotic-organized) (Understandability Dimension)												
Outer oriented	60	5.03	1.61	.21	1.12	.67	2.93	118	.004	2.93	117.60	.004
Inner-oriented	60	4.15	1.70	.22								
White Race(primitive-organized) (Understandability Dimension)												
Outer-oriented	60	5.43	1.42	.18	1.12	.67	1.81	118	.07	1.81	117.60	.07
Inner-oriented	60	4.95	1.50	.19								
Life(weak-strong) (Fear Dimension)												
Outer-oriented	60	5.90	.80	.10	1.63	.06	2.20	118	.01	2.60	111.60	.01
Inner-oriented	60	5.47	1.02	.13								
Life(nonfrightening-frightening) (Fear Dimension)												
Outer-oriented	60	3.48	1.62	.21	1.28	.34	-2.69	118	.008	-2.69	116.20	.008
Inner-oriented	60	4.23	1.43	.19								
Life(profane-sacred) (Evaluative Dimension)												
Outer-oriented	60	5.07	1.27	.16	1.57	.086	-2.14	118	.035	-2.14	112.50	.035
Inner-oriented	60	5.52	1.02	.13								

Cont. Table 6. Differences Between Outer and Inner-oriented Respondents in Specific Affective Meaning Responses to the Concepts

VARIABLES (Specific Affective Meanings) (DIMENSIONS)	n	M	SD	SE	F	p (two-tail)	Pooled Variance Estimate			Separate Variance Estimate		
							t	df	p	t	df	p
Life(primitive-civilized) (Evaluative Dimension)												
Outer-oriented	60	5.05	1.55	.20	1.12	.67	3.40	118	.001	3.40	117.70	.001
Inner-oriented	60	4.83	1.48	.19								
Life(dark-bright) (Evaluative Dimension)												
Outer-oriented	60	5.40	1.34	.17	1.21	.47	2.20	118	.03	2.20	116.98	.03
Inner-oriented	60	4.83	1.48	.19								
Life(mysterious-understandable) (Understandability Dimension)												
Outer-oriented	60	3.48	1.82	.24	2.15	.004	3.28	118	.001	3.28	104.17	.001
Inner-oriented	60	2.55	1.24	.16								
Life(strange-familiar) (Understandability Dimension)												
Outer-oriented	60	4.08	1.60	.21	1.31	.30	3.29	118	.001	3.29	115.92	.001
Inner-oriented	60	3.18	1.40	.18								
Life(chaotic-organized) (Understandability Dimension)												
Outer-oriented	60	4.58	1.61	.21	1.22	.44	2.92	118	.004	2.92	116.80	.004
Inner-oriented	60	3.77	1.45	.19								

Cont. Table 6. Differences Between Outer and Inner-oriented Respondents in Specific Affective Meaning Responses to the Concepts

VARIABLES (Specific Affective Meanings) (DIMENSIONS)	n	M	SD	SE	F	p (two-tail)	Pooled Variance Estimate			Separate Variance Estimate		
							t	df	p	t	df	p
Life(powerless-powerful) (Potency Dimension)												
Outer-oriented	60	5.65	1.07	.14	2.13	.004	3.13	118	.002	3.13	104.38	.002
Inner-oriented	60	4.88	1.56	.20								
Death(nonfrightening-frightening) (Fear Dimension)												
Outer-oriented	60	5.13	1.71	.22	1.57	.087	1.79	118	.076	1.79	112.50	.076
Inner-oriented	60	4.50	2.14	.28								
Death(dirty-clean) (Evaluative Dimension)												
Outer-oriented	60	4.20	1.73	.22	1.12	.66	-2.41	118	.017	-2.41	117.60	.017
Inner-oriented	60	4.98	1.31	.17								
Death(bad-good) (Evaluative Dimension)												
Outer-oriented	60	3.88	1.86	.24	1.03	.91	-2.47	118	.015	-2.47	117.97	.015
Inner-oriented	60	4.72	1.83	.24								
Death(dark-bright) (Evaluative Dimension)												
Outer-oriented	60	2.78	1.98	.26	1.20	.49	-2.82	118	.006	-2.82	117.05	.006
Inner-oriented	60	3.85	2.16	.28								
Waking State/Day (relaxed-tense) (Fear Dimension)												
Outer-oriented	60	3.53	1.56	.20	1.25	.40	-2.27	118	.025	-2.27	116.6	.025
Inner-oriented	60	4.22	1.74	.22								

Cont. Table 7.   Mean Scores for Each Stimulus Item (Concept) on The Semantic Differential

CONCEPTS	FEAR SCALES				EVALUATIVE SCALES					UNDERSTANDABILITY SCALES		POTENCY SCALE	
	Passive-Active	Weak-Strong	Relaxed-Tense	Nonfrightening-Frightening	Dirty-Clean	Profane-Sacred	Primitive-Civilized	Bad-Good	Dark-Bright	Mysterious-Understandable	Strange-Familiar	Chaotic-Organized	Powerless-Powerful
The Nature of the Unconscious/Me													
Outer-oriented	5.18	5.30	4.25	3.72	4.47	4.60	4.05	4.65	4.08	2.77	3.28	3.97	5.42
Inner-oriented	5.18	5.33	4.58	3.98	4.22	4.48	3.55	4.72	3.77	2.77	3.23	3.23	5.47
The Nature of God													
Outer-oriented	6.17	6.72	2.95	2.60	6.70	6.75	5.77	6.70	6.38	1.98	3.97	5.72	6.73
Inner-oriented	5.80	6.13	3.10	3.18	6.15	6.32	4.52	6.32	5.83	2.20	4.02	5.10	6.27
The Nature of Satan													
Outer-oriented	5.53	5.48	6.00	6.17	1.60	1.98	2.35	1.37	1.42	2.10	2.08	2.32	5.82
Inner-oriented	5.73	5.32	5.58	5.92	1.85	2.05	2.52	1.52	1.73	2.62	2.42	3.02	5.60
The Nature of the Waking State/Day													
Outer-oriented	5.23	5.05	3.53	2.47	5.07	4.30	530	5.13	5.02	5.42	5.60	5.12	5.17
Inner-oriented	5.35	4.88	4.22	3.00	4.98	4.33	4.98	4.85	5.13	4.88	5.22	4.10	4.67
The Nature of the Dream.State/Night													
Outer-oriented	5.70	5.50	4.52	4.23	4.22	4.35	3.20	4.63	3.57	2.28	3.05	2.92	5.33
Inner-oriented	5.48	5.38	4.12	4.53	4.08	4.08	2.95	4.52	3.38	2.10	2.58	2.88	5.28
The Nature of Life													
Outer-oriented	5.95	5.90	4.07	3.48	5.23	5.07	5.05	5.68	5.40	3.48	4.08	4.58	5.65
Inner-oriented	5.83	5.47	4.48	4.23	4.98	5.52	4.12	5.58	4.83	2.55	3.18	3.77	4.88
The Nature of Death													
Outer-oriented	3.63	5.12	4.17	5.13	4.20	5.38	3.80	3.88	2.78	2.08	2.23	4.30	5.27
Inner-oriented	3.45	5.45	3.50	4.50	4.98	5.78	3.40	4.72	3.85	2.08	2.55	4.58	5.70

Cont. Table 7.   *Mean Scores for Each Stimulus Item (Concept) on The Semantic Differential*

CONCEPTS	FEAR SCALES				EVALUATIVE SCALES					UNDERSTANDABILITY SCALES		POTENCY SCALE	
	Passive-Active	Weak-Strong	Relaxed-Tense	Nonfrightening-Frightening	Dirty-Clean	Profane-Sacred	Primitive-Civilized	Bad-Good	Dark-Bright	Mysterious-Understandable	Strange-Familiar	Chaotic-Organized	Powerless-Powerful
The Unknown													
Outer-oriented	4.58	5.07	5.00	5.20	4.05	4.32	3.25	3.77	2.75	1.71	1.88	3.23	5.47
Inner-oriented	4.10	5.55	4.83	5.10	4.22	4.75	3.15	4.47	3.28	1.50	1.90	3.20	5.57

oriented respondents. Overall, a significant difference was found between the two groups in their SD ratings regarding the Potency of the color "white." That is, overall the ratings by Outer-oriented respondents indicated that the color "white" was Highly Potent, while overall the SD ratings by Inner-oriented respondents indicated that they were Neutral or Ambivalent in this regard. Further, in terms of specific qualities or affective meanings, the SD ratings by Outer-oriented respondents indicated that the color "white" was significantly "powerful" and "strong" (as opposed to "Neutral" SD ratings by Inner-oriented respondents in regard to the powerless-powerful and weak-strong qualities), and was somewhat less "sacred" and "Neutral" in regard to a passive-active quality (as opposed to a SD rating of "A Tendency Toward passive" by Inner-oriented respondents). Both groups rated the color "black" on the SD as "frightening," "dark," "tense," "dirty," "primitive," and somewhat "profane" with a "Tendency Toward active" and rated the color "white" on the SD as "nonfrightening," "bright," "good," "clean," civilized," "understandable," "familiar," and "organized."

In terms of the race names, the difference between Outer-oriented respondents and Inner-oriented respondents nearly reached the level of significance in terms of their overall Evaluative responses to "The Black Race" (Outer, M=3.98, SD=1.10, SE=.14; Inner, M=4.28, SD=.91, SE=.12; t= -1.59, p < .11). That is, while evaluatively both groups basically gave Neutral or Ambivalent responses on the SD to "The Black Race" (perhaps due, in part, to Low Understandability), the SD ratings by Outer-oriented respondents were closer to a "Negative" direction and the SD ratings by Inner-oriented respondents were closer to a "Positive" direction. More specifically in terms of qualitative differences in affective meanings, while the SD ratings by Outer-oriented respondents were "Neutral" or "Ambivalent" toward "The Black Race" in terms of a profane-sacred quality or affective meaning and a bad-good quality or affective meaning, the SD ratings by Inner-oriented respondents indicated a "Tendency Toward good" and was closer to a "Tendency Toward sacred" rating for the concept "The Black Race." The SD rating by Outer-oriented respondents, however, indicated that they were closer to a "Tendency Toward dark" rating for "The Black Race" concept. These qualitative differences in affective meaning were significant or almost significant statistically. There was a significant difference found between the two groups in terms of their overall Evaluative responses connotatively and to some extent, in terms of their

Understandability responses to "The White Race" concept. That is, the SD ratings by Outer-oriented respondents indicated that "The White Race" was significantly more "Positive" and had somewhat Higher Understandability to them than the ratings by Inner-oriented respondents. In terms of specific qualitative differences in affective meanings, when compared to Inner-oriented respondents, the SD ratings by Outer-oriented respondents indicated that to them "The White Race" was significantly "brigher," "cleaner," more "civilized," "good" (as opposed to a "Neutral" rating by Inner-oriented respondents regarding the bad-good quality or affective meaning), "organized" (as opposed to a "Neutral" rating by Inner-oriented respondents regarding the chaotic-organized quality or affective meaning), with a "Tendency Toward sacred" (as opposed to a "Neutral" rating by Inner-oriented respondents regarding the profane-sacred quality or affective meaning). While the SD ratings by Outer-oriented respondents also indicated that "The Black Race" was "powerful" and "strange" with almost a "Tendency Toward chaotic," the SD ratings by both groups indicated that "The Black Race" was "tense," "active," and "strong," and that the "The White Race" was "nonfrightening," "active," "strong," "powerful," and "familiar."

   In terms of Consciousness vs the Unconscious, significant differences were found between Outer-oriented respondents and Inner-oriented respondents in terms of their overall Evaluative responses connotatively to "The Nature of Consciousness." That is, the SD ratings by Outer-oriented respondents indicated that "The Nature of Consciousness" overall was significantly more "Positive" and significantly more "Potent" to them than the ratings by Inner-oriented respondents. A significant difference was also found between the two groups regarding an overall Fear response to "The Nature of the Unconscious Portions of the Self." That is, the SD ratings by Inner-oriented respondents indicated a "Tendency Toward" High Fear for "The Nature of the Unconscious Portions of the Self," while the ratings by Outer-oriented respondents were "Neutral" or "Ambivalent" in this regard (almost an overall tendency toward High Fear response). In terms of specific qualitative differences in affective meanings, when compared to Inner-oriented respondents, the SD ratings by Outer-oriented respondents indicated that "The Nature of Consciousness" was somewhat more "powerful" and "stronger," somewhat more "understandable," significantly more "organized," and was somewhat "Neutral" in regard to a relaxed-tense quality or affective meaning (as opposed to a "Tendency Toward tense" rating by Inner-oriented respondents). Regarding specific qualities in affective meanings, when compared to Inner-oriented respondents, the SD ratings by Outer-oriented respondents indicated that to them "The Nature of the Unconscious" in general was "Neutral" in regard to a relaxed-tense quality or affective meaning (as opposed to a "Tendency Toward tense" rating by Inner-oriented respondents), and that "The Nature of the Unconscious Portions of the Self" to them was significantly less "active," significantly less "strong" and less "powerful," was somewhat more "Neutral" in regard to a primitive-civilized quality or affective meaning (almost a "Tendency Toward primitive" rating), and was somewhat "Neutral" in regard to a chaotic-organized quality or affective meaning (as opposed to a "Tendency Toward chaotic" rating by Inner-oriented respondents).

While the SD ratings by Inner-oriented respondents additionally indicated that "The Nature of Consciousness" had "a tendency toward clean," the ratings by both groups indicated that "The Nature of Consciousness" was "bright," "good," "active," "familiar," "civilized," somewhat "sacred," and somewhat "nonfrightening." In contrast to consciousness, while the SD ratings by Inner-oriented respondents additionally indicated that "The Nature of the Unconscious" in general was "frightening," "tense," with a "Tendency Toward chaotic," the ratings by both groups indicate that "The Nature of the Unconscious" in general was "active," "strong," "mysterious," "strange," "powerful," somewhat "primitive," somewhat "good," and somewhat "dark." In contrast to Consciousness, the ratings by both groups indicated that "The Nature of the Unconscious Portions of the Self" was "mysterious," "strange," and "dark." In contrast to Consciousness, while the SD ratings by Inner-oriented respondents indicated that "The Nature of the Unconscious Portions of Me" was slightly "tense" and "chaotic" and the ratings by Outer-oriented respondents indicated a "Tendency Toward sacred," the rating by both groups indicated that "The Nature of the Unconscious Portions of Me" was "active," "strong," "mysterious," and "powerful" with a "Tendency Toward strange."

In terms of "The Waking State (Day)" vs "The Dreaming State (Night)," a significant difference was found between Outer-oriented respondents and Inner-oriented respondents in terms of their overall Understandability responses to "The Nature of Waking State (Day)." That is, the SD ratings by Outer-oriented respondents indicated that "The Nature of the Waking State (Day)" concept overall connotively had significantly Higher Understandability to them than the SD ratings by Inner-oriented respondents. Regarding specific qualities or affective meanings, when compared to Inner-oriented respondents, the SD ratings by Outer-oriented respondents indicated that "The Nature of Waking State (Day)" was significantly more "understandable," "organized" (as opposed to a "Neutral" rating by Inner-oriented respondents regarding a chaotic-organized quality or affective meanings), somewhat more "powerful," and was "Neutral" in regard to a relaxed-tense quality or affective meaning (the rating by Inner-oriented respondents was closer to a "Tendency Toward relaxed"). No significant differences were found between the two groups in regard to their overall connotative responses to "The Nature of the Dreaming State (Night)" (the SD ratings by the two groups for "The Nature of the Dreaming State (Night)" nearly reached the level of significance in regard to quality "strange," Inner-oriented respondents appearing to acknowledge the quality or affective meaning moreso than Outer-oriented respondents). The SD ratings by Inner-oriented respondents also indicated that "The Nature of the Dreaming State" was somewhat "frightening," while the SD ratings by Outer-oriented respondents indicated that it had a "Tendency Toward tense." The SD ratings by both groups indicated that "The Nature of the Waking State," in varying degrees, was "nonfrightening," "active," "strong," "bright," "good," "clean," "civilized," and "familiar," and that "The Nature of the Dreaming State" was "active," "strong," "mysterious," "chaotic," and somewhat "primitive" with a "Tendency Toward dark" (to some extent) and a "Tendency Toward good."

In terms of the religious concepts, significant differences were found between Outer-oriented respondents and Inner-oriented respondents in terms of their overall Evaluative responses and overall Potency responses connotatively to "The Nature of God" and their overall Understandability responses connotatively to "The Nature of Satan." That is, the SD ratings by Outer-oriented respondents indicated that "The Nature of God" overall was significantly more "Positive" and significantly more "Potent" to them than the SD ratings by Inner-oriented respondents, and that "The Nature of Satan" overall had significantly Less Understandability to them than the ratings by Inner-oriented respondents. Regarding specific qualities or affective meanings, when compared to Inner-oriented respondents, the SD ratings by Outer-oriented respondents indicated that

"The Nature of God" was significantly "brighter," "cleaner," more "sacred," more "civilized," more "good," "stronger," and somewhat more "nonfrightening," more "organized," and more "powerful," and that "The Nature of Satan" was significantly more "chaotic." The SD ratings by both groups indicated that "The Nature of God" was "active," "relaxed," and "mysterious," and "The Nature of Satan" was "dark," "bad," "profane," "primitive," "mysterious," "strange," "active," and "powerful."

In terms of the concepts of Life and Death, significant differences were found between Outer-oriented respondents and Inner-oriented resondents in terms of their overall Understandability responses, their overall Potency responses and to some extent their overall Evaluative responses connotatively to "The Nature of Life," and in terms of their overall Evaluative responses connotatively to "The Nature of Death." That is, the SD ratings by Outer-oriented respondents indicated that "The Nature of Life" overall was significantly more "Potent" and somewhat more "Positive" than the ratings by Inner-oriented respondents. Further, while the SD ratings by Outer-oriented respondents were "Neutral" or "Ambivalent" overall connotatively in regard to an Understandability response, the SD ratings by Inner-oriented respondents indicated that "The Nature of Life" concept overall evoked a response significantly closer to a "Tendency Toward" Low Understandabilty. Also, while the SD ratings by Outer-oriented respondents were "Neutral" or "Ambivalent" overall connotatively in regard to an Evaluative response to "The Nature of Death," the SD ratings by Inner-oriented respondents indicated that "The Nature of Death" concept overall slightly evoked a "Tendency Toward Positive" response for them and this difference between the two groups was significant. Regarding specific qualities or affective meanings, when compared to Inner-oriented respondents, the SD ratings by Outer-oriented respondents indicated that "The Nature of Life" was significantly "brighter," "stronger," less "sacred," "civilized" (as opposed to a "Neutral" rating by Inner-orieinted respondents regarding a primitive-civilized quality or affective meaning), less "mysterious," more "powerful," with a "Tendency Toward nonfrightening" (as opposed to a "Neutral" rating by Inner-oriented respondents regarding a nonfrightening-frightening quality or affective meaning), a "Tendency Toward organized" (as opposed to a "Neutral" rating by Inner-oriented respondents regarding a chaotic-organized quality or affective meaning), and was "Neutral" in regard to a strange-familiar quality or affective meaning (as opposed to a "Tendency Toward strange" rating by Inner-oriented respondents). Significantly, when compared to Inner-oriented respondents, the SD ratings by Outer-oriented respondents indicated that "The Nature of Death" was "dark" (as opposed to a "Neutral" rating by Inner-oriented respondents regarding a dark-bright quality), somewhat more "frightening," and was "Neutral" in regard to a dirty-clean quality or affective meaning (as opposed to a "Tendency Toward clean" rating by Inner-oriented respondents) and a good-bad quality or affective meaning (as opposed to a "Tendency Toward good" rating by Inner-oriented respondents). The SD ratings by both groups indicated that "The Nature of Life" was "good," "active," and "clean" and that "The Nature of Death" was "strong," "powerful," and "strange." The SD ratings by Inner-oriented respondents also indicated that "The Nature of Life" was close to a "Tendency Toward tense" and that "The Nature of Death" was "passive," "relaxed," and "sacred" with a "Tendency Toward primitive and organized."

In terms of "The Unknown," there was a significant difference (at $p < .10$) between Outer-oriented respondents and Inner-oriented respondents in terms of their overall Evaluative responses connotatively to "The Unknown." That is, while evaluatively both groups responded neutrally or ambivalently regarding "The Unknown," the SD ratings by Outer-oriented respondents overall indicated that "The Unknown" was significantly closer to a "Tendency Toward a Negative" response than the ratings Inner-oriented respondents. Regarding specific qualities or affective meanings, the SD ratings by Outer-oriented respondents indicated that "The Unknown" concept was somewhat "darker" and significantly less "strong" than the ratings by Inner-oriented respondents. Further, while interpretively the SD ratings by both groups were "Neutral" or "Ambivalent" in regard to a bad-good quality or affective meaning for "The Unknown," the ratings by Outer-oriented respondents were significantly closer to a "Tendency Toward bad" and the ratings by Inner-oriented respondents were significantly closer to a "Tendency Toward good." The SD ratings by both groups indicated that "The Unknown" was "frightening," "strange," "mysterious," "primitive," "tense," "strong," and "powerful." The SD ratings by Inner-oriented respondents also indicated that "The Unknown" evoked a "Tendency Toward sacred" response for them, while the ratings by Outer-oriented respondents also indicated that "The Unknown" evoked a "Tendency Toward active" response for them.

Overall, then, it was found that, in many instances, Outer-oriented respondents and Inner-oriented respondents did deal with the various concepts in significantly different ways (validation for part of Hypothesis 1-b). The dimension, however, on which the concept or construct was being considered, as well as the specific quality or affective meaning associated with a given concept, was important. That is, on some dimension, there may have been an overall Neutral response, but when specific qualities or affective meanings on a given dimension were examined, there may have been significant differences in the respective responses of the two groups. Further, while both groups may have had similar overall connotative responses on a given dimension or in reference to a given quality or affective meaning, there was a significant difference between the two groups in terms of the relative intensity of their responses.

Of particular interest here were the findings that Outer- and Inner-oriented respondents reacted differentially to "The Black Race" and "The White Race" in terms of affective meanings. That is, in regard to "The Black Race," the SD ratings by Outer-oriented respondents overall were closer to a "Negative" direction with some "High Fear" qualities or affective meanings involved, while the ratings by Inner-oriented respondents overall were closer to a "Positive" direction with some "High Fear" qualities or affective meanings involved. In contrast, the SD ratings by Outer-oriented respondents for "The White Race" overall were significantly more "Positive" and indicated somewhat Higher Understandability than the ratings by Inner-oriented respondents. The "dark-bright" quality also tended to be somewhat pronounced for Outer-oriented respondents, but not for Inner-oriented respondents in regard to the race names. In fact, for Outer-oriented respondents, the *common qualities* or *affective meanings* for a "black-Black Race-Unconscious" association were "active," "strong," "powerful," and a "Tendency Toward dark" (or a Neutral SD rating closer to a "Tendency Toward dark"). For Inner-oriented respondents, the *common qualities* or *affective meanings* for this association were "active," "strong," and "tense," but not "dark" (or less of a close rating here). The SD ratings by Inner-oriented respondents also indicated that "The Black Race" and "The Nature of the Unconscious" shared the common quality or affective meaning "good." In regard to a "white-White Race-Consciousness" association, the *common qualities* or *affective meanings* indicated by Outer-oriented respondents were "bright," "good," "nonfrightening," "sacred," "civilized," "clean," "understandable," "organized," "familiar," "strong," and "powerful." For Inner-oriented respondents, the *common qualities* or *affective meanings* for this association were "bright," "clean," "nonfrightening," "familiar," "understandable," and "civilized." The findings, therefore, indicate a connection of the above associations to the "color code" via affective meanings, with some indication that Outer-oriented respondents may be a little more intense in their use of the dark-bright quality. These findings lend some support to Hypothesis 1-a.

Finally, in terms of affective meanings, there was evidence that overall the concepts "The Black Race," "The Nature of the Unconscious," "The Nature of the Dreaming State," "The Nature of Death," "The Nature of Satan," and "The Unknown" tended to have specific qualities (affective meanings) more in common with the color "black" and overall the concepts "The White Race," "The Nature of Consciousness," "The Nature of the Waking State," "The Nature of Life," and "The Nature of God" tended to have specific qualities (affective meanings) more in common with the color "white." In terms of specific qualities (affective meanings), some polarizing among the contrasting subsets of concepts was evident, particularly in regard to the "dark-bright" quality, the "bad-good" quality, and the "primitive-civilized" quality. While these tendencies were found for both Outer- and Inner-oriented respondents, the color-coding occurred slightly more for Outer-oriented respondents than for Inner-oriented respondents when specific qualities (affective meanings) were examined (e.g., except for "The Nature of the Unconscious/Me" item for Outer-oriented respondents, but not for as many stimulus items for Inner-oriented respondents, the "dark" quality or affective meaning tended to occur for all stimulus items on the former subset of concepts and the "bright" quality or affective meaning for all stimulus items on the latter subset). The findings, therefore, tended to further support Hypothesis 1-a.

Comparative Fear Responses For Race-linked and Non Race-linked Projective Stories

Tests of significance (t-tests) were used to determine the statistical significance of the differences between Outer- and Inner-oriented respondents in terms of the Level of Fear experienced (indicated) by respondents while writing the four Projective Stories. As mentioned in the Methods section, Story 1 involved writing a brief story about a boss of employees, while Story 3 involved writing a brief story about a Black boss of White employees; Story 2 involved writing a brief story about a couple, while Story 4 involved writing a brief story about a Black-White interracial couple. The Fear Thermometer measured Levels of Fear that were experienced (indicated) in relation to the tasks *Before, During,* and *After.*

In general, Hypothesis 2 predicted that there would be a difference between Outer-oriented respondents and Inner-oriented respondents in terms of the Level of Fear that would be experienced (indicated) when these respective respondents were engaged in induced projective activities such as story writing. More specifically, Hypothesis 2 predicted that, in this instance, Outer-oriented respondents may experience a higher Level of Fear but would indicate a lower Level of Fear since they tend to reject emotions. It was further predicted that overall when the Black Race was a factor, the Level of Fear would increase.

It should be noted that, in this study, "*After* (Story 1)" was equivalent to "*Before* (Story 2)," "*After* (Story 2)" was equivalent to "*Before* (Story 3)," and "*After* (Story 3)" was equivalent to "*Before* (Story 4)" with respect to the Level of Fear that was measured.

Table 8 reflects an analysis of differences between Outer- and Inner-oriented respondents, based on mean differences (t-tests) *Before, During,* and *After* writing the Projective Stories. Overall, the findings indicated that there were significant differences between the two groups *After* Story 1 ($t = -2.44$, $p < .016$) and somewhat *After* Story 2 ($t = -1.92$, $p < .057$), Story 3 ($t = -1.89$, $p < .06$), and Story 4 ($t = -1.85$, $p < .067$). In each of these instances, the overall mean score for Outer-oriented respondents was lower than the mean score for Inner-oriented respondents after writing the four stories. This was also true where the differences were clearly not statistically significant (i.e., *Before* and *During* for each story). As partially predicted, then, it was found that Outer-oriented respondents did indicate a

Table 8   **Comparison of the Levels of Fear Indicated By Outer- vs Inner-**
Oriented Respondents in Relation to Writing Four Projective Stories

Story 1	M	SD	t	p (two-tail)
Before				
Outer-oriented	3.55	2.15	-0.20	N.S.
Inner-oriented	3.63	2.38		
During				
Outer-oriented	3.80	2.24	1.15	N.S
Inner-oriented	4.30	2.53		
Atter				
Outer-oriented	2.60	1.64	2.44	.02
Inner-oriented	3.47	2.21		
Story 2				
During				
Outer-oriented	4.00	2 55	1.00	N.S.
Inner-oriented	4.48	2 74		
After				
Outer-oriented	3.03	2.08	-1.92	.06
Inner-Oriented	3.85	2.55		
Story 3				
During				
Outer-oriented	4.07	2.65	-1.11	N.S.
Inner-oriented	4.62	2.77		
Atter				
Outer-oriented	3.13	2.17	-1.89	.06
Inner-oriented	3.98	2.72		
Story 4				
During				
Outer-oriented	4.28	2.68	-1.21	N.S
Inner-oriented	4.88	2.76		
Atter				
Outer-oriented	3.23	2.38	-1.85	.07
Inner-oriented	4.08	2.64		

significantly lower Level of Fear than Inner-oriented respondents *After* the writing of each of the projective stories. As implied in Hypothesis 2, what this finding could mean is that Inner-oriented respondents were more willing to reflect on their feelings *After* the experience of writing the Projective Stories, whereas Outer-oriented respondents tended to reject their emotions. The above finding is consistent with the earlier finding of how each group tended to describe itself (i.e., Inner-oriented respondents as "Feeling Types" and Outer-oriented respondents as "Thinking Types"), how each group tended to "indicate" their respective state anxiety (i.e., Outer-oriented respondents tended to indicate a lower state anxiety), and also consistent with Murray's characterization of an Inner- (intraceptive) vs an Outer-(extraceptive) oriented person.

The following four Projective Stories by an Outer-oriented respondent further illustrate the above interpretation:

Story 1 (Boss of Employees)
"John (the boss) is sitting inside his office watching his employees. He is thinking that deep down he favors some employees over others & feels guilty about this; he sees no way of solving this problem. John's employees see him watching them. They get very uptight about this. Even though he tries to be like close friends to them, they still see him as the boss & worry about what he thinks of them & watch their actions while he is around."

Story 2 (Couple)
"Donna & Jim have just come back from school. Donna is a professor at the school while Jim is a student. They have had an ongoing relationship for a few weeks now. Jim has longed for Donna for quite awhile & Donna has been looking for someone who is understanding, young & innocent. They enter the bedroom & quickly embrace. They undress each other and then have sex on the bed but both seem a bit unsatisfied afterwards. They don't know what they want."

<u>Story 3</u> (Black Boss of White Employees)

"John is the boss, in fact, just became the boss quite recently. He & two of his good friends were up for the job & he got it. All 3 of them feel he received it because he is black. His two white friends think that the decision to make him boss was because of his color was wrong & are a bit mad & hateful towards John. They wanted the job! John also wanted the job & knows or at least thinks he got it because of his color. This makes him quite uncomfortable & he does not know what to do about it."

<u>Story 4</u> (Black-White Interracial Couple)

"Tom & Marianne have been married for over a year & are still having problems (not big but still troublesome). Tom is black & his wife is white. Since their marriage, neither of each other's parents will talk with them but they now seem to be softening a bit. The biggest problem is not between the couple but the way others look at them. This makes them each feel uncomfortable & makes their relationship a bit strained."

It is clear, then, that this Outer-oriented person exhibited a fair amount of anxiety in the four stories. In fact, this anxiety is similar to, if not greater than the anxiety expressed by Inner-oriented respondents. Evidence supporting this pattern is provided by additional data in a later section, which reports how judges evaluated the Level of Fear expressed in the content of the various Projective Stories (i.e., more "high" than "low"). Nevertheless, Outer-oriented respondents indicated a significantly lower Level of Fear *After* the writing of each of the Projective Stories. The findings, in part, support the general thrust of Hypothesis 2.

When the Level of Fear was examined more closely *Before, During,* and *After* writing the Projective Stories, it was observed that it increased from *Before* to *During,* decreased from *During* to *After,* and changed from *Before* to *After* in all cases. To explore the patterns observed for each group further in terms of the effect of an Outer-Inner orientation, an analysis of variance was used to determine the significance of this effect in terms of the increases (*Before* vs *During*), decreases (*During* vs *After*), and changes (*Before* vs *After*) in Level of Fear as respondents wrote the Projective Stories. As can be seen in Table 9, there was a significant effect of the Outer-Inner orientation variable only in terms of the *Before* vs *After*

Table 9. *Analysis of Variance of the Effect of the Outer-Inner Orientation Scores on the Level of Fear Indicated by Respondents Before vs During, Before vs After, and During vs After the Writing of the Four Projective Stories*

LEVEL OF FEAR–BEFORE VS. DURING

BY ORIENTATION	STORY 1				STORY 2			
Source of Variation	df	MS	F	p (two-tail)	df	MS	F	p (two-tail)
Main Effects								
Outer-Inner Orientation	1	5.21	.96	.33	1	4.41	1.10	.296
Explained	1	5.21	.96	.33	1	4.41	1.10	.296
Residual	118	5.45			118	3.995		
Total	119	5.44			119	3.998		

LEVEL OF FEAR–BEFORE VS. DURING

BY ORIENTATION	STORY 3				STORY 4			
Source of Variation	df	MS	F	p (two-tail)	df	MS	F	p (two-tail)
Main Effects								
Outer-Inner Orientation	1	2.13	.38	.54	1	1.86	.34	.56
Explained	1	2.13	.38	.54	1	1.86	.34	.56
Residual	118	5.67			118	5.45		
Total	119	5.64			119	5.42		

LEVEL OF FEAR–BEFORE VS. AFTER

BY ORIENTATION	STORY 1				STORY 2			
Source of Variation	df	MS	F	p (two-tail)	df	MS	F	p (two-tail)
Main Effects								
Outer-Inner Orientation	1	18.41	5.085	.026	1	.075	.028	.87
Explained	1	18.41	5.085	.026	1	.075	.029	.87
Residual	118	6.62			118	2.635		
Total	119	3.74						

Table 9. (Cont.) Analysis of Variance of the Effect of the Outer-Inner Orientation Scores on the Level of Fear Indicated by Respondents Before vs During, Before vs After, and During vs After the Writing of the Four Projective Stories

LEVEL OF FEAR–BEFORE VS. AFTER

BY ORIENTATION	STORY 3				STORY 4			
Source of Variation	df	MS	F	p (two-tail)	df	MS	F	p (two-tail)
Main Effects								
Outer-Inner Orientation	1	.03	.009	.92	1	0.0	0.0	1.0
Explained	1	.03	.009	.92	1	0.0	0.0	1.0
Residual	118	3.596			118	4.02		
Total	119	3.57			119	3.99		

LEVEL OF FEAR–DURING VS. AFTER

BY ORIENTATION	STORY 1				STORY 2			
Source of Variation	df	MS	F	p (two-tail)	df	MS	F	p (two-tail)
Main Effects								
Outer-Inner Orientation	1	4.03	1.53	.22	1	3.33	1.31	.29
Explained	1	4.03	1.53	.22	1	3.33	1.31	.29
Residual	118	2.64			118	2.95		
Total	119	2.66			119	2.95		

LEVEL OF FEAR–DURING VS. AFTER

BY ORIENTATION	STORY 3				STORY 4			
Source of Variation	df	MS	F	p (two-tail)	df	MS	F	p (two-tail)
Main Effects								
Outer-Inner Orientation	1	2.70	.98	.32	1	1.875	.45	.51
Explained	1	2.70	.98	.32	1	1.875	.45	.51
Residual	118	2.74			118	4.19		
Total	119	2.74			119	4.17		

Level of Fear indicated for Story 1 (F = 5.08, p < .026). That is, there was a significant effect of the person's Outer vs Inner orientation (i.e., a significant difference between the two groups) in terms of a change in Level of Fear from *Before* to *After* as a result of dealing with power without regard to race.

For Outer-oriented respondents and Inner-oriented respndents, respectively, tests of significance (t-tests) were used to determine whether or not the general patterns of increase (*Before* vs *During*), decrease (*During* vs *After*), and change (*Before* vs *After*) in Levels of Fear were significant as general shifts for each group. As can be seen in Table 10, for Outer-oriented respondents, the Level of Fear did increase significantly from *Before* to *During* the writing of the Projective Stories (except for Story 1), did decrease significantly from *During* to *After* the writing of each story, and changed significantly from *Before* to *After* the writing of Stories 1 and 2, but not the writing of Stories 3 and 4. That is, when dealing with power without regard to race, the Level of Fear for Outer-oriented respondents did not increase significantly from *Before* to *During* the experience, but did increase significantly when dealing with Black-White power relations; in both instances, the Level of Fear decreased significantly from *During* to *After* the experience. When dealing with intimacy, both with and without regard to the Black Race, the Level of Fear for Outer-oriented respondents significantly increased from *Before* to *During* the experience and also significantly decreased from *During* to *After*. Interestingly, however, Outer-oriented respondents did not indicate a significant change in Level of Fear from *Before* to *After* when the Black Race was a factor in regard to power and intimacy, but the Level of Fear was significantly lower *After* the experience than *Before* when dealing with power without regard to race and was significantly higher *After* the experience than *Before* when dealing with intimacy without regard to race.

For Inner-oriented respondents, the Level of Fear increased significantly from *Before* to *During* the writing of each of the stories, decreased significantly from *During* to *After* the writing of each of the stories, but did not change significantly from *Before* to *After* the writing of any of the stories. That is, when dealing with power and intimacy, with and without regard to the Black Race, the Level of Fear for Inner-oriented respondents increased significantly from *Before* to *During* the experience, decreased significantly from *During* to *After*, but overall did

Table 10.   Comparison of Significant Differences Before vs After, Before vs During, and During vs After in terms of the Levels of Fear Indicated by Outer-oriented Respondents (Ss) and Inner-oriented Respondents (Ss) in Writing Four Projective Stories.

	Outer-Oriented Ss					**Inner-Oriented Ss**				
					p (two-					p (two-
STORY 1	M	SD	Comparison	t	tail)	M	SD	Comparison	t	tail)
Before	3.55	2.15	Before vs After	3.61	.001	3.63	2.38	Before vs After		.73 .45
During	3.80	2.24	Before vs During	-0.76	.45	4.30	2.53	Before vs During	-2.46	.017
After	2.60	1.64	During vs After	5.72	.001	3.47	2.21	During vs After	3.97	.001
STORY 2										
Before	2.60	1.64	Before vs After	-2.94	.005	3.47	2.21	Before vs After	-1.49	.14
During	4.00	2.55	Before vs During	-5.59	.001	4.48	2.74	Before vs During	-3.83	.001
After	3.03	2.08	During vs After	4.03	.001	3.85	2.55	During vs After	3.14	.003
STORY 3										
Before	3.03	2.08	Before vs After	-0.52	.61	3.85	2.55	Before vs After	-0.47	.64
During	4.07	2.65	Before vs During	-3.70	.001	4.62	2.77	Before vs During	-2.30	.025
After	3.13	2.17	During vs After	4.42	.001	3.98	2.72	During vs After	2.93	.005
STORY 4										
Before	3.13	2.17	Before vs After	-0.46	.65	3.98	2.72	Before vs After	-0.34	.74
During	4.28	2.68	Before vs During	-3.98	.001	4.88	2.76	Before vs During	-2.87	.006
After	3.23	2.38	During vs After	4.09	.001	4.08	2.64	During vs After	2.94	.005

not change from *Before* to *After* as a result of the experience of writing any of the stories.

To look more closely at the impact of the Black Race factor in regard to projection and Levels of Fear, Levels of Fear indicated for Story 1 (Boss of Employees) were compared to Levels of Fear indicated for Story 3 (Black Boss of White Employees) and Levels of Fear indicated for Story 2 (Couple) were compared to Levels of Fear indicated for Story 4 (Black-White Interracial Couple). These comparisons were made for both Outer-oriented respondents and Inner-oriented respondents. Tests of significance (t-tests) were used to make the comparisons of the Levels of Fear *Before*, *During*, and *After* the writing of the Projective Stories.

As can be seen in Table 11, for Outer-oriented respondents, the Level of Fear *Before* dealing with Black-White power relations was somewhat lower (at the $p < .10$ level) in a significant way than the Level of Fear *Before* dealing with power without regard to race. However, for Outer-oriented respondents, the Level of Fear

Table 11. **Comparison of the Levels of Fear When the Black Race was a Factor (Story 3, Story 4) vs Not a Factor (Story 1, Story 2) for Outer-oriented Respondents and Inner-oriented Respondents in Writing Four Projective Stories.**

Time of Measurement	Outer-oriented Ss				Inner-Oriented Ss			
	M	SD	t	p (two tail)	M	SD	t	p (two tail)
Before								
Story 1	3.55	2.15	1.68	.097	3.63	2.38	-0.80	.43
Story 3	3.03	2.08			3.85	2.55		
During								
Story 1	3.80	2.24	-1.33	.19	4.30	2.53	-1.34	.19
Story 3	4.07	2.65			4.62	2.77		
After								
Story 1	2.60	1.64	-2.77	.007	3.45	2.21	-2.01	.049
Story 3	3.13	2.17			3.98	2.72		
Before								
Story 2	2.60	1.64	-2.77	.007	3.45	2.21	-2.01	.049
Story 4	3.13	2.17			3.98	2.72		
During								
Story 2	4.00	2.55	-1.20	.23	4.48	2.74	-1.43	.16
Story 4	4.28	2.68			4.88	2.76		
After								
Story 2	3.03	2.08	-0.86	.39	3.85	2.55	-0.80	.43
Story 4	3.23	2.38			4.08	2.64		

After dealing with Black-White power relations was significantly higher than the Level of Fear *After* dealing with power without regard to race. For Outer-oriented respondents, no significant difference between dealing with Black-White power relations and dealing with power without regard to race was found in terms of the Level of Fear indicated *During* the experience of writing the stories. Further, for Outer-oriented respondents, the Level of Fear *Before* dealing with Black-White interracial intimacy was significantly higher than the Level of Fear *Before* dealing with intimacy without regard to race. And finally, for Outer-oriented respondents, no significant difference between dealing with Black-White interracial intimacy and dealing with intimacy without regard to race was found in terms of the Level of Fear indicated *During* and *After* the experience.

For Inner-oriented respondents, the Level of Fear *After* dealing with Black-White power relations was significantly higher than the Level of Fear *After* dealing with power without regard to race. The Level of Fear *Before* dealing with Black-White interracial intimacy, then, was significantly higher than the Level of Fear *Before* dealing with intimacy without regard to race. For Inner-oriented respondents, no significant difference between dealing with Black-White power relations and dealing with power without regard to race was found in terms of the Level of Fear indicated *Before* and *During* the experience of writing the stories. Further, for Inner-oriented respondents, no significant difference between dealing with Black-White interracial intimacy and dealing with intimacy without regard to race was found in terms of the Level of Fear indicated *During* and *After* the experience of writing the stories.

The findings suggest, then, that when projection is induced (experienced) and the Black Race is a factor in relation to power and intimacy, the Level of Fear is somewhat higher *After* a Black-White power experience and that there may be a carry over of Fear when intimacy is an issue. In other words, the Level of Fear is influenced significantly afterwards for respondents in general, irrespective of the Outer or Inner orientation and primarily in relation to Black-White power relations. These findings thus partially support Hypothesis 2.

Comparative Fear Responses On the Multifactor Racial Attitude Inventory (MRAI)

Tests of significance were used to determine the significant differences between Outer- and Inner-oriented respondents in terms of Level of Fear experienced (indicated) by respondents while completing the MRAI. The MRAI was an inventory involving attitudes toward the Black Race. In general, Hypothesis 2 further predicted that there would be a difference between Outer-oriented respondents and Inner-oriented respondents in terms of the Level of Fear that would be indicated when these respective respondents were engaged in induced projective activities such as expressing an attitude about an object (attitude-confrontation). It was predicted that overall when the Black Race was a factor, the Level of Fear would increase, particularly in regard to this attitude-confrontation experience since it relates directly to the Black Race.

In terms of attitude-confrontation when the Black Race was a factor (MRAI), then, it was again observed that for Outer-oriented respondents and Inner-oriented respondents, the Level of Fear increased from *Before* to *During* the MRAI experience, decreased from *During* to *After* the MRAI experience, and for Inner-oriented respondents changed from *Before* to *After* the MRAI experience. As can be seen in Table 12, there were no significant differences between Outer-oriented respondents and Inner-oriented respondents in terms of the Level of Fear that they indicated *Before*, *During*, or *After* the MRAI experience. Further, there were no significant differences between Outer-oriented respondents and Inner-oriented respondents in terms of an indicated increase in Level of Fear from *Before* to *During* the MRAI experience, an indicated decrease in Level of Fear from *During* to *After* the MRAI experience, or an indicated change in Level of Fear from *Before* to *After* the MRAI experience. However, as can be seen on Table 13, for both groups the Level of Fear did increase significantly from *Before* to *During* the MRAI experience, did decrease significantly from *During* to *After* the MRAI experience, but did not change significantly from *Before* to *After* the MRAI experience. Again, the general thrust of Hypothesis 2 is partially supported.

Table 12. Analysis ·*of Variance of the Effect of the Outer-Inner Orientation Scores on the Level of Fear Indicated by Ss Before, During, and After and Before vs During, Before vs After, and During vs After In Relation to the Multiracial Attitude Inventory (MRAI).*

LEVEL OF FEAR IN RELATION TO THE MRAI

By Orientation	Before vs During				Before vs After				During vs After			
Source of	df	MS	F	p	df	MS	F	p	df	MS	F	p
Main Effects Outer-Inner Orientation	1	2.41	.63	.43	1	1.20	.25	.62	1	.21	.07	.79
Explained	1	2.41	.63	.43	1	1.20	.25	.62	1	.21	.07	.79
Residual	118	3.803			118	4.81			118	2.99		
Total	119	3.79			119	4.78			119	2.97		

LEVEL OF FEAR IN RELATION TO THE MRAI

By Orientation	Before				During				After			
Source of	df	MS	F	p	df	MS	F	p	df	MS	F	p
Main Effects Outer-Inner Orientation	1	.41	.07	.79	1	.83	.13	.72	1	.21	.04	.84
Explained	1	.41	.07	.79	1	.83	.13	.72	1	.21	.04	.84
Residual	118	5.59			118	6.64			118	5.14		
Total	119	5.55			119	6.59			119	5.10		

Table 13. *Comparison of the Levels of Fear Indicated by Outer- vs Inner-Oriented Respondents (Ss) in Relation to the MRAI as Measured at Different Times in the Attitude-Confrontation Experience.*

GROUP	M	SD	Comparison	t	p (two tail)
Outer-oriented Ss					
Before	3.55	2.17	Before vs During	-3.65	.001
During	4.43	2.48	Before vs After	0.00	1.00
After	3.55	2.15	During vs After	4.67	.001
Inner-oriented Ss					
Before	3.43	2.54	Before vs During	-5.44	.001
During	4.70	2.67	Before vs After	-0.76	.45
After	3.63	2.38	During vs After	4.54	.001

Comparatively, as can be seen on Figure 1, the Level of Fear for Outer-oriented respondents was actually slightly higher than the Level of Fear for Inner-oriented respondents *Before* the MRAI experience. *During* the MRAI experience, however, the Level of Fear indicated by Outer-oriented respondents was slightly lower than the Level of Fear indicated by Inner-oriented respondents. Interestingly, *After* the MRAI experience, the Level of Fear for Outer-oriented respondents actually dropped slightly lower than the Level of Fear for Inner-oriented respondents. A general impression, then, in accord with Hypothesis 2, is that Outer-oriented respondents tended to reject their emotions *During* the MRAI experience and appeared to be much more relieved *After* the MRAI experience. Inner-oriented respondents, however, appeared to be more willing to acknowledge their anxiety *During* the MRAI experience and appeared to be a bit more reflective about their emotions *After* the MRAI experience. Of course, as indicated above, these observed differences were not statistically significant.

Figure 1. **Levels of Fear indicated by Outer-oriented and Inner-oriented Respondents (Ss) Before, During, and After the MRAI Experience.**

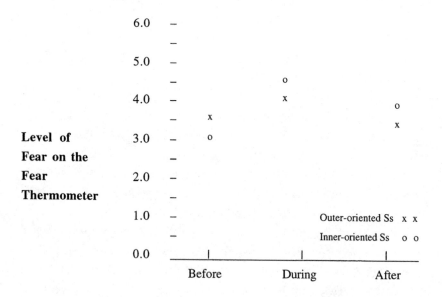

MRAI Experience

Attitudes Toward Blacks

Tests of significance (t-tests) were used to examine the effect of an Outer vs Inner orientation and differences between Outer- vs Inner-oriented respondents in terms of their attitudes toward Blacks as measured on the MRAI. As can be seen on Table 14, then, there was a significant effect of an Outer vs Inner orientation in terms of an Anti-black Disposition for (1) Ease in Interracial Contacts (F = 6.85, p < .01), (2) Private Rights (F = 6.72, p < .01), and somewhat for (3) Integration-Segregation Policy (F = 3.28, p < .07), (4) Black Inferiority (F = 3.36, p < .079), (5) Local Autonomy (F = 3.62, p < .06), and (6) Gradualism (F = 3.46, p < .065). That is, Outer-oriented respondents and Inner-oriented respondents had significantly different responses in regard to the above attitude dimensions involving the Black race. No significant differences were found between the two groups in terms of their respective attitudes regarding Acceptance in Close Personal Relationships, Subtle Derogatory Beliefs, Acceptance in Status Superior Relationships, and Black Superiority.

Table 14. Analysis of Variance of the Effect of the Outer-Inner Orientation Scores on Anti-Black Dispositions as Measured by the Multifactor Racial Attitude Inventory (MRAI).

ANTI-BLACK DISPOSITIONS (MULTIRACIAL ATTITUDES)

By Orientation Source of Variation	Integration-Segregation Policy				Acceptance in Close Personal Relations				Black Inferiority			
	df	MS	F	p	df	MS	F	p	df	MS	F	p
Main Effects Outer-Inner Orientation	1	16.13	3.28	.07	1	.41	.14	.71	1	8.01	3.36	.069
Explained	1	16.13	3.28	.07	1	.41	.14	.71	1	8.01	3.36	.069
Residual	118	4.92			118	2.90			118	2.39		
Total	119	5.01			119	2.88			118	2.43		

Table 14 (Cont.) Analysis of Variance of the Effect of the Outer-Inner Orientation Scores on Anti-Black Dispositions as Measured by the Multifactor Racial Attitude Inventory (MRAI).

ANTI-BLACK DISPOSITIONS (MULTIRACIAL ATTITUDES)

By Orientation Source of Variation	Ease In Interracial Contacts				Subtle Derogatory Beliefs				Local Autonomy			
	df	MS	F	p	df	MS	F	p	df	MS	F	p
Main Effects Outer-Inner Orientation	1	48.13	6.85	.01	1	1.01	.23	.63	1	26.13	3.62	.06
Explained	1	48.13	6.85	.01	1	1.01	.23	.63	1	26.13	3.62	.06
Residual	118	7.03			118	4.38			118	7.23		
Total	19	7.37			119	4.35			119	7.39		

ANTI-BLACK DISPOSITIONS (MULTIRACIAL ATTITUDES)

By Orientation Source of Variation	Acceptance in Status-Superior Relations				Private Rights				Gradualism			
	df	MS	F	p	df	MS	F	p	df	MS	F	p
Main Effects Outer-Inner Orientation	1	2.70	1.19	.28	1	28.03	6.72	.01	1	29.01	3.46	.065
Explained	1	2.70	1.19	.28	1	28.03	6.72	.01	1	29.01	3.46	.065
Residual	118	2.27			118	4.17			118	8.38		
Total	119	2.27			119	4.37			119	8.55		

ANTI-BLACK DISPOSITIONS (MULTIRACIAL ATTITUDES)

By Orientation Source of Variation	Black Superiority (A Social Desirability Measure)			
	df	MS	F	p
Main Effects Outer-Inner Orientation	1	7.50	1.38	.24
Explained	1	7.50	1.38	.24
Residual	118	5.45		
Total	119	5.57		

Except for the Black Superiority measure on the MRAI, which was used as a social desirability measure, the lower the mean score, the more Anti-black the tendency was for the attitude dimension. As can be seen in Table 15, then, when compared to Inner-oriented respondents, Outer-oriented respondents had significantly more of an Anti-black Disposition (at either $p < .05$ or $p < .10$) in terms of attitudes about the use of Segregation-Integration Policies to address inequities between the races, the Inferiority of the Black Race, Ease in Interracial Contact with the Black Race, the use of the idea of Local Autonomy to justify discrimination in regard to the Black Race, the use of the idea of Private Rights to avoid addressing inequities between the races, and the use of the idea of Gradualism to avoid addressing inequities between the races.

In addition to the findings above, it was also observed that Inner-oriented respondents tended to score higher than Outer-oriented respondents on all of the attitude dimensions, indicating a tendency on the part of the former group to be less Anti-black in its disposition. Overall, the lowest mean scores (i.e., highest Anti-black Disposition) for both Outer- and Inner-oriented respondents tended to occur in regard to "Ease in Interracial Contacts" and "Gradualism," and respondents in both groups tended to give relatively honest responses and not simply socially desirable responses. The above findings validate part of Hypothesis 3 which predicted that there would be a difference between Outer- and Inner-oriented respondents generally in regard to Anti-black Disposition and specifically in regard to the kind of attitudes each group had toward the Black Race.

Table 15. Comparison of Outer-oriented Respondents (Ss) and Inner-Oriented Respondents (Ss) (i.e., Test of Significant Differences) in terms of their Anti-Black Dispositions (Attitudes Towards Blacks on the MRAI)

VARIABLE (Attitude)	M	SD	t	p (two-tail)
Integration-Segregation Policy				
Outer-oriented Ss	7.52	2.39	-1.81	.07
Inner-oriented Ss	8.25	2.03		

Table 15 (Cont.) Comparison of Outer-oriented Respondents (Ss) and Inner-Oriented Respondents (Ss) (i.e., Test of Significant Differences) in terms of their Anti-Black Dispositions (Attitudes Towards Blacks on the MRAI)

VARIABLE (Attitude)	M	SD	t	p (two-tail)
Acceptance in Close Personal Relationships				
Outer-oriented Ss	9.17	1.78	-0.38	.71
Inner-oriented Ss	9.28	1.63		
Black Inferiority				
Outer-oriented Ss	7.85	1.56	-1.83	.07
Inner-oriented Ss	8.37	1.53		
Ease In Interracial Contacts				
Outer-oriented Ss	3.22	2.52	-2.62	.01
Inner-oriented Ss	4.48	2.78		
Subtle Derogatory Beliefs				
Outer-oriented Ss	5.73	1.87	-0.48	.63
Inner-oriented Ss	5.92	2.29		
Local Autonomy				
Outer-oriented Ss	4.95	2.78	-1.90	.06
Inner-oriented Ss	5.88	2.59		
Private Rights				
Outer-oriented Ss	6.50	2.15	-2.59	.01
Inner-oriented Ss	7.47	1.93		
Acceptance in Status-Superior Relationships				
Outer-oriented Ss	9.02	1.42	-1.09	.28
Inner-oriented Ss	9.32	1.59		
Gradualism				
Outer-oriented Ss	3.08	2.51	-1.86	.06
Inner-oriented Ss	4.07	3.23		
Black Superiority				
Outer-oriented Ss	2.13	1.86	-1.17	.24
Inner-oriented Ss	2.63	2.73		

Ethnocentrism and Underlying Feeling States

To examine Outer- vs Inner-oriented respondents in terms of their Ethnocentrism and Underlying Feeling States, three judges used Levinson's (1950) manual and judged each respondent's responses to the two Projective Questions as described above in the Methods section. The three judges had varying degrees of clinical experience. Judge 1 had the most clinical experience (psychologist; director of a child guidance clinic); judge 2 had some clinical experience (counselor); and judge 3 was a psychology intern. The manual allowed the judges to classify Ss' responses to each of the questions as "Low" Ethnocentric or "High" Ethnocentric and to link the response(s) to a description of an Underlying Feeling State for the response(s). Using this scheme, Outer-oriented respondents were compared to Inner-oriented respondents as each judge perceived the differences and similarities. Frequency profile measures (see Table 16), as well as significance tests (t-tests), were used to compare the two groups as each judge perceived them.

As can be seen in Table 17, for both Outer- and Inner-oriented respondents, all three judges basically found a significant difference in how the respondents responded to Projective Questions 1 and 2 in terms of Ethnocentrism. That is, most responses to Projective Question 1 were categorized as "Low" Ethnocentric responses and most responses to Projective Question 2 were categorized as "High" Ethnocentric responses. In terms of Underlying Feeling States associated with the "Low" and "High" Ethnocentric responses for Projective Questions 1 and 2, overall the three judges varied somewhat in finding significant differences in this regard for each of the groups. Despite some variation among the judges, there was some agreement that the Underlying Feeling States associated with the "High" Ethnocentric responses for Projective Questions 1 and 2 tended to be significantly different (see Table 17).

Overall, then, the three judges generally found no significant difference between Outer-oriented respondents and Inner-oriented respondents in terms of their Ethnocentrism with slight variations regarding the association of Underlying Feeling States. Projective Question 1 ("Moods") generally tended to generate "Low" Ethnocentric responses, while Projective Question 2 ("Drive Nuts") generally tended to generate "High" Ethnocentric responses, irregardless of the respodents' Outer or Inner orientation. There also seemed to be agreement among

Table 16. Frequency Profiles Regarding Projective Questions Based on the Scoring of Three Judges.

Judge 1	Outer-oriented Ss			Inner-oriented Ss		
	Freq.	Adj. %	Cum. %	Freq.	Adj. %	Cum. %
Category (Question #1)						
Low Ethnocentric	39	65	65	41	68	68
High Ethnocentric	20	33	98	19	32	100
No Response	1	2	100			
Description–Low Ethnocentric						
Conscious Conflict & Guilt	30	50	50	38	63	63
Focal Dependency & Love Seeking	9	15	65	3	5	68
Description–High Ethnocentric						
Violations of Conventional Values	3	5	5	2	3	3
Threatening, Nonsupporting Environment	11	18	23	13	22	25
Rumblings from Below	6	10	33	4	7	32
Category (Question #2)						
Low Ethnocentric	10	17	17	13	22	22
High Ethnocentric	48	80	97	47	78	100
No Response	2	3	100			
Description–Low Ethnocentric						
Inner Psychological States	9	15	15	11	19	19
Dominating, Blocking, Rejecting Environment	1	2	17	2	3	22

Table 16 (Cont.)   *Frequency Profiles Regarding Projective Questions Based on the Scoring of Three Judges.*

Judge 1	Outer-oriented Ss			Inner-oriented Ss		
	Freq.	Adj. %	Cum. %	Freq.	Adj. %	Cum. %
Description–High Ethnocentric						
Rumblings from Below	26	43	43	29	48	48
Threatening, Irritating, Nonsupporting Environment	21	35	78	18	30	78
Combined the Two Above	1	2	80			
Judge 2						
Category Question #1)						
Low Ethnocentric	47	76	76	45	75	75
High Ethnocentric	10	17	93	12	20	95
High & Low Trends Equal	3	7	100	3	5	100
Description–Low Ethnocentric						
Conscious Conflict & Guilt (CCG)	22	37	37	29	48	48
Focal Dependency & Love Seeking (FDLS)	4	7	42	3	5	53
Open Hostility by Self or Others Toward Love Object (OHSOTLO)	1	2	44	1	2	55
Ambiguous	2	3	47			
Equal Trends	1	2	49			
Combined CCG & FDLS	8	13	62	3	5	60
Combined CCG & OHSOTLO	7	12	74	6	10	70

Table 16 (Cont.)   *Frequency Profiles Regarding Projective Questions Based on the Scoring of Three Judges.*

Judge 2	Outer-oriented Ss			Inner-oriented Ss		
	Freq.	Adj. %	Cum. %	Freq.	Adj. %	Cum. %
Description–Low Ethnocentric (Cont.)						
Combined FDLS & OHSOTLO	2	3	76	3	5	75
Description–High Ethnocentric						
Violations of Conventional Values (VCV)	5	8	8	3	5	5
Threatening, Nonsupporting Environment (TNE)	2	3	11	5	8	13
Rumblings from Below (RFB)	1	2	13	1	2	15
Ambiguous	2	3	17			
Combined TNE & RFB				2	3	18
Combined VCV & RFB				1	2	20
Category (Question #2)						
Low Ethnocentric	22	37	37	19	32	32
High Ethnocentric	30	50	87	30	50	82
No Response/ Ambiguous	8	13	100	11	18	100

Table 16 (Cont.)   *Frequency Profiles Regarding Projective Questions Based on the Scoring of Three Judges.*

Judge 2	Outer-oriented Ss Freq.	Adj. %	Cum. %	Inner-oriented Ss Freq.	Adj. %	Cum. %
Description–Low Ethnocentric						
Inner Psychological States	9	15	15	9	15	15
Dominating, Blocking, Rejecting Environment	10	17	32	3	5	20
Combined the Above	3	5	37	7	12	32
Description–High Ethnocentric						
Rumblings from Below	9	15	15	12	20	20
Threatening, Irritating, Nonsupporting Environment	14	23	38	12	20	40
Combined the Above	7	12	50	6	10	50
Judge 3						
Category (Question #1)						
Low Ethnocentric	43	72	72	42	70	70
High Ethnocentric	17	28	100	17	28	98
No Response/ Ambiguous				1	2	100

Table 16 (Cont.)   *Frequency Profiles Regarding Projective Questions Based on the Scoring of Three Judges.*

Judge 3	Outer-oriented Ss			Inner-oriented Ss		
	Freq.	Adj. %	Cum. %	Freq.	Adj. %	Cum. %
Description–Low Ethnocentric						
Conscious Conflict & Guilt (CCV)	27	46	46	28	47	47
Focal Dependency & Love Seeking (FDLS)	12	20	66	4	7	54
Open Hostility by Self or Others Toward Love Object (OHSOTLO)	2	3	69	1	2	56
Combined CCG & FDLS	2	3	72	6	10	66
Combined CCG & OHSOTLO				2	3	68
Combined FDLS & OHSOTLO				1	2	70
Description–High Ethnocentric						
Violations of Conventional Values (VCV)	5	8	8	6	10	10
Threatening, Irritating, Nonsupporting Environment (TINE)	7	12	20	8	13	23
Rumblings from Below	3	5	25	3	5	28
Combined VCV & TINE	1	2	27			
No Response	1	2	28			

Table 16 (Cont.)   *Frequency Profiles Regarding Projective Questions Based on the Scoring of Three Judges.*

Judge 3 Category (Question #2)	Outer-oriented Ss			Inner-oriented Ss		
	Freq.	Adj. %	Cum. %	Freq.	Adj. %	Cum. %
Low Ethnocentric	18	30	30	17	28	28
High Ethnocentric	40	67	97	42	70	98
No Response	2	3	100	1	2	100
Description–Low Ethnocentric						
Inner Psychological States (IPS)	9	15	15	12	20	20
Dominating, Blocking, Rejecting, Environment (DBRE)	9	15	30	5	8	28
Description–High Ethnocentric						
Rumblings from Below (RFB)	22	37	37	26	43	43
Threatening, Irritating, Nonsupportive Environment (TINE)	15	25	62	15	25	68
Combined RFB & TINE	1	2	64			
No Response	2	3	67			

Table 17. Tests of Significance in Regard to the Categorization of Ethnocentric Responses by Outer-oriented Respondents and Inner-oriented Respondents and Underlying Feeling States Associated with Low and High Ethnocentric Responses.

Judge 1	Outer-oriented Ss			Inner-oriented Ss		
	M	t	p (two tail)	M	t	p (two tail)
Categorization of Ethnocentric Responses						
Question #1	1.33	-7.55	.001	1.32	-7.19	.001
Question #2	1.83			1.78		
Underlying Feeling States						
Low Ethnocentric for Question #1	1.40			1.23		
		1.41	.19		.43	.67
Low Ethnocentric for Question #2	1.10			1.15		
High Ethnocentric for Question #1	2.10			2.11		
		2.80	.01		2.70	.015
High Ethnocentric for Question #2	1.58			1.61		
Judge 2						
Categorization of Ethnocentric Responses						
Question #1	1.31	-2.10	.04	1.26	-4.10	.001
Question #2	1.57			1.62		
Underlying Feeling States						
Low Ethnocentric for Question #1	3.24			2.81		
		2.50	.02		-1.17	.125
Low Ethnocentric for Question #2	1.40			3.63		
High Ethnocentric for Question #1	3.10			3.73		
		.66	.53		2.23	.05
High Ethnocentric for Question #2	2.50			2.27		

Table 17 (Cont.) Tests of Significance in Regard to the Categorization of Ethnocentric Responses by Outer-oriented Respondents and Inner-oriented Respondents andUnderlying Feeling States Associated with Low and High Ethnocentric Responses.

Judge 3	Outer-oriented Ss			Inner-oriented Ss		
	M	t	p (two tail)	M	t	p (two tail)
Categorization of Ethnocentric Responses						
Question #1	1.29	-5.39	.001	1.29	-5.51	.001
Question #2	1.69			1.72		
Underlying Feeling States						
Low Ethnocentric for Question #1	1.33			2.80		
		-1.46	.16		-2.17	.048
Low Ethnocentric for Question #2	1.89			1.60		
High Ethnocentric for Question #1	2.15			2.00		
		2.67	.02		2.10	.005
High Ethnocentric for Question #2	1.31			1.43		

the judges that there was an overall difference in the Underlying Feeling States associated with "High" Ethnocentric responses that were stimulated by "Things that Drive People Nuts" and those that were stimulated by a person's "Moods." The findings in regard to Ethnocentrism, then, did not support Hypothesis 3, though there was an unexpected finding in terms of what tends to generate "High" and "Low" Ethnocentric responses for respondents.

Manifest Projective Content of Four Stories: An Evaluation

The three judges also evaluated the manifest content of the four Projective Stories. They used a manual that was developed in such a way as to allow them to examine the stories for what characters were *Thinking, Feeling,* and *Doing* in the stories, for the *Outcome* of the stories, and for the Level of Fear judged to be in the manifest content of the stories. *"Thinking"* generally referred to the degree to which there was internal vs. external conflict or tension depicted in the story and whether or not the conflict or tension was "inside" the individual(s), in the relationship itself among the characters, and/or in the external context or situation. *"Feeling"* referred to whether the *Affect* in the story was mostly positive, mostly negative, mostly mixed, or unclear. *"Doing"* generally referred to the *Movement* in the story, either toward coming together, separating, or some combination of the two (e.g., coming together followed by separating; separating followed by coming together). *"Outcome"* generally referred to how the story ended (that is, if characters actually came together or separated at the end of the story and whether or not this happened positively or negatively or whether there was no clear resolution). And finally, *"Level of Fear"* referred to a rating by each judge regarding the Level of Fear judged to be in the manifest content of the story, (i.e., not at all high, not high, high or very high).

Table 18 provides a summary of comparisons regarding the manifest projective content for each story as each judge saw it for Outer-oriented respondents vs Inner-oriented respondents in terms of the respective *Thinking, Feeling, Doing (Movement), Outcome,* and *Level of Fear.* Also compared in Table 18 are Story 1 (Boss of Employees) vs Story 3 (Black Boss of White Employees) and Story 2 (Couple) vs Story 4 (Black-White Interracial Couple) for Outer-oriented Respondents and Inner-oriented Respondents in terms of significant differences in *Thinking, Feeling, Doing, Outcome,* and *Level of Fear* as each judge saw it.

As can be seen in Table 18, at $p < .10$, all three judges saw significant differences between Outer-oriented respondents and Inner-oriented respondents in terms of the *Feelings* depicted when dealing with the issue of power without regard to race.

Table 18. *Comparisons of Outer-oriented Respondents vs Inner-oriented Respondents in terms of the Manifest Projective Content of Four Stories as Scored by Three Judges for Thinking, Feeling, Doing (Movement), Outcome, and Level of Fear.*

Judge 1	Outer M	SD	Inner M	SD	t	p (two-tail)	Comparisons	t	p (two-tail)
Thinking									
Story 1	4.83	2.23	4.27	1.82	1.53	.13	Outer-Stories 1 vs 3	.73	.47
Story 2	4.20	2.53	3.63	1.92	1.38	.17	Outer-Stories 2 vs 4	-4.94	.001
Story 3	4.60	2.39	4.15	2.07	1.10	.27	Inner-Stories 1vs 3	1.07	.29
Story 4	6.05	2.31	5.88	1.98	.42	.67	Inner-Stories 2 vs 4	-6.34	.001
Feeling									
Story 1	2.82	1.88	2.37	.94	1.66	.10	Outer-Stories 1 vs 3	1.22	.23
Story 2	2.58	1.99	2.33	1.29	1.14	.26	Outer-Stories 2 vs 4	-1.96	.055
Story 3	2.62	1.94	2.55	1.58	.21	.84	Inner-Stories 1 vs 3	.09	.93
Story 4	2.90	1.90	2.55	1.52	1.11	.27	Inner-Stories 2 vs 4	-1.07	.29
Doing									
Story 1	3.25	2.22	2.47	1.42	2.30	.02	Outer-Stories 1 vs 3	-0.32	.75
Story 2	3.00	2.29	2.47	1.69	1.45	.15	Outer-Stories 2 vs 4	.42	.68
Story 3	3.33	2.23	3.00	1.93	.88	.38	Inner-Stories 1 vs 3	-1.50	.14
Story 4	2.88	2.40	2.82	2.05	.16	.87	Inner-Stories 2 vs 4	-1.14	.26
Outcome									
Story 1	3.45	2.29	2.85	1.66	1.65	.10	Outer-Stories 1 vs 3	-0.28	.78
Story 2	3.13	2.34	2.77	1.84	.96	.34	Outer-Stories 2 vs 4	1.11	.27
Story 3	3.53	2.27	3.12	2.06	1.05	.29	Inner-Stories 1 vs 3	-0.47	.64
Story 4	2.82	2.39	2.68	2.09	.33	.75	Inner-Stories 2 vs 4	.56	.58
Fear Level									
Story 1	2.82	1.80	2.55	.68	1.07	.29	Outer-Stories 1 vs 3	-1.35	.18
Story 2	2.77	1.82	2.57	1.11	.73	.47	Outer-Stories 2 vs 4	-0.32	.75
Story 3	2.92	1.74	2.67	1.36	.88	.38	Inner-Stories 1 vs 3	1.06	.29
Story 4	2.80	1.78	2.87	1.28	-0.24	.82	Inner-Stories 2 vs 4	-1.89	.06
Judge 2									
Thinking									
Story 1	4.68	2.49	4.18	1.94	1.23	.22	Outer-Stories 1 vs 3	1.28	.21
Story 2	4.18	2.68	3.67	2.24	1.15	.25	Outer-Stories 2 vs 4	-5.69	.001
Story 3	4.25	2.30	3.88	2.29	.87	.38	Inner-Stories 1 vs 3	1.70	.09
Story 4	6.55	2.51	6.50	2.03	.12	.91	Inner-Stories 2 vs 4	-8.29	.001
Feeling									
Story 1	2.53	1.94	2.02	.73	1.94	.057	Outer-Stories 1 vs 3	1.57	.12
Story 2	2.23	2.02	1.83	1.18	1.32	.19	Outer-Stories 2 vs 4	-0.10	.92
Story 3	2.30	1.96	2.33	1.76	-0.10	.92	Inner-Stories 1 vs 3	0.00	1.00
Story 4	2.25	2.02	1.93	1.53	.97	.34	Inner-Stories 2 vs 4	.12	.90
Doing									
Story 1	2.82	2.10	2.45	1.32	1.14	.26	Outer-Stories 1 vs 3	0.00	1.00
Story 2	2.43	2.15	2.37	1.50	.20	.84	Outer-Stories 2 vs 4	2.56	.013
Story 3	2.82	2.06	2.62	1.90	.55	.58	Inner-Stories 1 vs 3	.71	.48
Story 4	1.92	2.13	2.13	1.85	-0.59	.55	Inner-Stories 2 vs 4	1.62	.11

Table 18 (Cont). *Comparisons of Outer-oriented Respondents vs Inner-oriented Respondents in terms of the Manifest Projective Content of Four Stories as Scored by Three Judges for Thinking, Feeling, Doing (Movement), Outcome, and Level of Fear.*

	Outer		Inner			p (two-tail)	Comparisons	t	p (two-tail)
Judge 2	M	SD	M	SD	t				
Outcome									
Story 1	3.03	2.28	2.75	1.64	.78	.44	Outer-Stories 1 vs 3	-0.41	.69
Story 2	2.70	2.35	2.48	1.81	.57	.57	Outer-Stories 2 vs 4	2.03	.048
Story 3	3.15	2.30	2.87	2.23	.69	.49	Inner-Stories 1 vs 3	.62	.54
Story 4	2.18	2.24	2.17	1.95	.04	.97	Inner-Stories 2 vs 4	1.46	.15
Fear Level									
Story 1	3.30	1.81	3.01	1.00	1.06	.29	Outer-Stories 1 vs 3	1.20	.24
Story 2	2.85	1.93	2.83	1.34	.05	.96	Outer-Stories 2 vs 4	-0.11	.91
Story 3	3.12	1.84	2.95	1.68	.52	.61	Inner-Stories 1 vs 3	2.35	.02
Story 4	2.87	1.86	3.08	1.38	-0.73	.47	Inner-Stories 2 vs 4	-0.92	.36
Judge 3									
Thinking									
Story 1	4.37	2.32	3.78	1.82	1.53	.13	Outer- Stories 1 vs 3	2.00	.05
Story 2	3.70	2.49	3.65	2.17	.12	.91	Outer-Stories 2 vs 4	-6.66	.001
Story 3	3.90	2.09	3.90	2.10	0.00	1.00	Inner-Stories 1 vs 3	.53	.60
Story 4	6.47	2.59	6.38	2.24	.19	.85	Inner-Stories 2 vs 4	-8.13	.001
Feeling									
Story 1	2.58	1.68	2.15	.76	1.82	.07	Outer-Stories 1 vs 3	.83	.41
Story 2	2.55	1.96	2.25	1.30	.99	.33	Outer-Stories 2 vs 4	-1.16	.25
Story 3	2.58	1.88	2.58	1.71	0.00	1.00	Inner-Stories 1 vs 3	-0.88	.38
Story 4	2.73	1.87	2.45	1.46	.93	.36	Inner-Stories 2 vs 4	-0.75	.46
Doing									
Story 1	2.63	1.86	2.60	1.18	.12	.91	Outer-Stories 1 vs 3	-0.08	.93
Story 2	2.93	2.13	2.52	1.61	1.21	.23	Outer-Stories 2 vs 4	-1.27	.21
Story 3	2.75	2.00	3.03	1.75	-0.83	.41	Inner-Stories 1 vs 3	-0.66	.52
Story 4	3.23	2.24	2.78	1.98	1.17	.25	Inner-Stories 2 vs 4	-0.71	.48
Outcome									
Story 1	3.00	2.06	2.85	1.59	.45	.66	Outer-Stories 1 vs 3	.40	.69
Story 2	2.73	2.27	2.43	1.74	.81	.42	Outer-Stories 2 vs 4	-0.24	.81
Story 3	3.03	2.23	2.77	2.07	.68	.50	Inner-Stories 1 vs 3	1.58	.12
Story 4	2.80	2.29	2.80	2.06	0.00	1.00	Inner-Stories 2 vs 4	-1.08	.28
Fear Level									
Story 1	2.95	1.63	2.78	.80	.71	.48	Outer-Stories 1 vs 3	-1.43	.16
Story 2	2.85	1.91	2.72	1.21	.46	.65	Outer-Stories 2 vs 4	-2.49	.016
Story 3	3.22	1.79	3.02	1.62	.64	.52	Inner-Stories 1 vs 3	.73	.47
Story 4	3.23	1.75	3.15	1.36	.29	.77	Inner-Stories 2 vs 4	-2.46	.017

When the manifest content of the Projective Stories was compared by each judge with regard to the Black Race factor (Story 1 vs Story 3; Story 2 vs Story 4) for Outer-oriented respondents and Inner-oriented respondents separately, all three judges indicated that for both Outer- and Inner-oriented respondents, there was a difference in the *Thinking* that occurred in relation to the issue of intimacy without regard to race vs Black-White interracial intimacy. For two judges, there was also an apparent difference for Inner-oriented respondents regarding the *Level of Fear* assessed to be in the above content. The three judges varied in their assessment of other significant differences of other aspects of the content of the stories (i.e., *Feelings*, *Outcomes*, etc.) for both groups of respondents.

To better understand the meaning of the above differences and further explore more subtle differences, profiles reflecting the actual breakdown of frequencies and percentages of the scoring for each judge regarding the manifest projective content were determined (see Table 19).

As can be seen in Table 19, in terms of the *Thinking* depicted for Story 1 (Boss of Employees), the three judges indicated that Outer- and Inner-oriented respondents tended to depict (experience or project) conflict/tension primarily in the boss-employee relationship itself when power without regard to race was an issue. Though they varied in their assessment of the degree of conflict/tension, the three judges also indicated that for Inner-oriented respondents, there was more internal conflict/tension than external conflict/tension and two judges further indicated that there was more internal conflict/tension for Outer-oriented respondents when power without regard to race was an issue.

In terms of the *Thinking* depicted for Story 2 (Couple), at least two judges indicated that Outer-oriented respondents depicted (experienced or projected) conflict/tension primarily as conflict/tension in the relationship itself when intimacy without regard to race was an issue. Though the judges varied somewhat in their assessment of the degree of internal vs external conflict/tension that was present, there was a tendency among the three judges to indicate that there was slightly more internal than external conflict/tension for Outer-oriented respondents. For Inner-oriented respondents, at least two judges indicated that these respondents tended to depict (experience or project) a relatively equal amount of conflict/tension in the relationship itself, as well as internal conflict/tension (though they varied with

Table 19.   *Summary of Frequencies and Percentages of the Scoring by Three Judges Regarding the Manifest Projective Content of Each of Four Stories for Outer-oriented Respondents and Inner-oriented Respondents.*

| | STORY 1 | | | | | | STORY 2 | | | | | |
| | Outer | | | Inner | | | Outer | | | Inner | | |
Judge 1	Freq	Adj %	Cum %	Freq	Adj %	Cum %	Freq	Adj %	Cum %	Freq	Adj %	Cum %
Thinking												
NNN	7	12	12	7	12	12	13	22	22	10	17	17
SNN	1	2	13	1	2	13				2	3	20
SNS	9	15	28	13	22	35	17	28	50	25	42	62
NNS	7	12	40	9	15	50	5	8	58	3	5	67
SSS	17	28	68	18	30	80	10	17	75	13	22	88
SSN	3	5	73	4	7	87	1	2	77	2	3	92
NSS	9	15	88	6	10	97	4	7	83	1	2	93
NSN	3	5	93	2	3	100	6	10	93	3	5	98
No Response	4	7	100				4	7	100	1	2	100
Feeling												
Mostly +	11	18	18	13	22	22	21	35	35	21	35	35
Mostly -	18	30	48	18	30	52	11	18	53	12	20	55
Mixed	22	37	85	23	38	90	20	33	87	24	40	95
Unclear	5	8	93	6	10	100	4	7	93	2	3	98
No Response	4	7	100				4	7	100	1	2	100
Doing												
Primarily CT	16	27	27	16	27	27	24	40	40	23	38	38
Primarily S	14	23	50	24	40	67	9	15	55	16	27	65
Primarily S/CT	7	12	62	8	13	80	4	7	62	5	8	73
Primarily CT/S	1	2	63				5	8	70	6	10	83
Unclear Move-												
ment	18	30	93	12	20	100	14	23	93	9	15	98
No Response	4	7	100				4	7	100	1	2	100
Outcome												
Came Together												
Positively	23	38	38	25	42	42	28	47	47	28	47	47
Came Together												
Negatively				1	2	43						
Separated												
Positively	2	3	42	2	3	47	2	3	50	4	7	53
Separated												
Negatively	13	22	63	22	37	83	12	20	70	18	30	83
No Resolution	18	30	93	10	17	100	14	23	93	9	15	98
No Response	4	7	100				4	7	100	1	2	100
Fear Level												
Not at all High	4	7	7	4	7	7	7	12	12	7	12	12
Not High	30	50	57	21	35	42	25	42	53	19	32	43
High	19	32	88	33	55	97	23	38	92	32	53	97
Very High	3	5	93	2	3	100	1	2	93	1	2	98
No Response	4	7	100				4	7	100	1	2	100

Table 19 (Cont.) Summary of Frequencies and Percentages of the Scoring by Three Judges Regarding the Manifest Projective Content of Each of Four Stories for Outer-oriented Respondents and Inner-oriented Respondents.

Judge 1	STORY 3 Outer Freq	Adj %	Cum %	STORY 3 Inner Freq	Adj %	Cum %	STORY 4 Outer Freq	Adj %	Cum %	STORY 4 Inner Freq	Adj %	Cum %
Thinking												
NNN	10	17	17	10	17	17	6	10	10	2	3	3
SNN				1	2	18	2	3	13	2	3	7
SNS	10	17	33	11	18	37				5	8	15
NNS	10	17	50	12	20	57	2	3	17	1	2	17
SSS	13	22	72	15	25	82	9	15	32	15	25	42
SSN				2	3	85	14	23	55	11	18	60
NSS	9	15	87	5	8	93	4	7	62	7	12	72
NSN	4	7	93	2	3	97	19	32	93	15	25	97
No Response	7	7	100	2	3	100	4	7	100	2	3	100
Feeling												
Mostly +	16	27	27	16	27	27	13	22	22	17	28	28
Mostly -	19	32	58	15	25	52	11	18	40	7	12	40
Mixed	17	28	87	19	32	83	25	42	82	32	53	93
Unclear	4	7	93	8	13	97	7	12	93	2	3	97
No Response	4	7	100	2	3	100	4	7	100	2	3	100
Doing												
Primarily CT	16	27	27	16	27	27	31	52	52	26	43	43
Primarily S	13	22	48	15	25	52	5	8	60	7	12	55
Primarily S/CT	5	8	57	9	15	67				4	7	62
Primarily CT/S	3	3	62	1	2	68	4	7	67	6	10	72
Unclear Movement	19	32	93	17	28	97	16	27	93	15	25	97
No Response	4	7	100	2	3	100	4	7	100	2	3	100
Outcome												
Came Together Positively	22	37	37	25	42	42	34	57	57	33	55	55
Came Together Negatively				1	2	43						
Separated Positively				2	3	47	2	3	60	2	3	58
Separated Negatively	16	27	63	14	23	70	7	13	72	11	18	77
No Resolution	18	30	93	16	27	97	13	22	93	12	20	97
No Response	4	7	100	2	3	100	4	7	100	2	3	100
Fear Level												
Not at all High	3	5	5	4	7	7	4	7	7	1	2	2
Not High	23	38	43	26	43	50	29	48	55	20	33	35
High	30	50	93	26	43	93	22	37	92	35	58	93
Very High				2	3	97	1	2	93	2	3	97
No Response	4	7	100	2	3	100	4	7	100	2	3	100

Table 19 (Cont.)   *Summary of Frequencies and Percentages of the Scoring by Three Judges Regarding the Manifest Projective Content of Each of Four Stories for Outer-oriented Respondents and Inner-oriented Respondents.*

| | STORY 1 | | | | | | STORY 2 | | | | | |
| | Outer | | | Inner | | | Outer | | | Inner | | |
Judge 2	Freq	Adj %	Cum %	Freq	Adj %	Cum %	Freq	Adj %	Cum %	Freq	Adj %	Cum %
Thinking												
NNN	6	10	10	6	10	10	12	20	20	11	18	18
SNN	8	13	23	4	7	17	9	15	35	12	20	38
SNS	7	12	35	9	15	32	6	10	45	6	10	48
NNS	14	23	58	24	40	72	13	22	67	17	28	77
SSS	1	2	60	2	3	75	1	2	68	2	3	80
SSN	6	10	70	7	12	87	2	3	72	1	2	82
NSS	7	12	82	2	3	90	6	10	82	6	10	92
NSN	7	12	93	6	10	100	7	12	93	4	7	98
No Response	4	7	100				4	7	100	1	2	100
Feeling												
Mostly +	17	28	28	13	22	22	29	48	48	26	43	43
Mostly -	20	33	62	35	58	80	14	23	72	24	40	83
Mixed	17	28	90	10	17	97	11	18	90	9	15	98
Unclear	2	3	93	2	3	100	2	3	93			
No Response	4	7	100				4	7	100	1	2	100
Doing												
Primarily CT	18	30	30	17	28	28	31	52	52	25	42	42
Primarily S	16	27	57	19	32	60	8	13	65	7	12	53
Primarily S/CT	12	20	77	11	18	78	7	12	77	14	23	77
Primarily CT/S	3	5	82	6	10	88	8	13	90	13	22	98
Unclear Movement	7	12	93	7	12	100	2	3	93			
No Response	4	7	100				4	7	100	1	2	100
Outcome												
Came Together Positively	26	43	43	24	40	40	33	55	55	31	52	52
Came Together Negatively	3	5	48	5	8	48	4	7	62	3	5	57
Separated Positively	5	8	57	5	8	57	2	3	65	6	10	67
Separated Negatively	11	18	75	14	23	80	6	10	75	10	17	83
No Resolution	11	18	93	12	20	100	11	18	93	9	15	98
No Response	4	7	100				4	7	100	1	2	100
Fear Level												
Not at all High	6	10	10	7	12	12	14	23	23	11	18	18
Not High	12	20	30	8	13	25	13	22	45	11	18	37
High	20	33	63	22	37	62	21	35	80	20	33	70
Very High	18	30	93	23	38	100	8	13	93	17	28	98
No Response	4	7	100				4	7	100	1	2	100

Table 19 (Cont.)   Summary of Frequencies and Percentages of the Scoring
by Three Judges Regarding the Manifest Projective Content of Each of
Four Stories for Outer-oriented Respondents and Inner-oriented
Respondents.

	STORY 3						STORY 4					
	Outer			Inner			Outer			Inner		
		Adj	Cum		Adj	Cum		Adj	Cum		Adj	Cum
Judge 2	Freq	%	%	Freq	%	%	Freq	%	%	Freq	%	%
Thinking												
NNN	7	12	12	8	13	13	5	8	8	2	3	3
SNN	7	12	23	11	18	32	4	7	15	3	5	8
SNS	6	10	33	8	13	45	1	2	17			
NNS	24	40	73	20	33	78	4	7	23	7	12	20
SSS	1	2	75	1	2	80						
SSN	3	5	80	1	2	82	2	3	27	13	22	42
NSS	3	5	85	3	5	87	7	12	38	6	10	52
NSN	5	8	93	5	8	95	33	55	93	27	45	97
No Response	4	7	100	3	5	100	4	7	100	2	3	100
Feeling												
Mostly +	23	38	38	19	32	32	29	48	48	29	48	48
Mostly -	20	33	72	23	38	70	13	22	70	18	30	78
Mixed	13	22	93	12	20	90	12	20	90	11	18	97
Unclear				3	5	95	2	3	93			
No Response	7	7	100	3	5	100	4	7	100	2	3	100
Doing												
Primarily CT	16	27	27	21	35	35	47	78	78	38	63	63
Primarily S	18	30	57	10	17	52	1	2	80	2	3	67
Primarily S/CT	13	22	78	19	32	83	2	3	83	7	12	78
Primarily CT/S	3	5	83	3	5	88	6	10	93	8	13	92
Unclear Move-ment	6	10	93	4	7	95				3	5	97
No Response	4	7	100	3	5	100	4	7	100	2	3	100
Outcome												
Came Together Positively	25	42	42	30	50	50	41	68	68	40	67	67
Came Together Negatively	4	7	48	2	3	53	4	7	75	1	2	68
Separated Positively	1	2	50	3	5	58	3	5	80	5	8	77
Separated Negatively	13	22	72	8	13	72	3	5	85	5	8	85
No Resolution	13	22	93	14	23	95	5	8	93	7	12	97
No Response	4	7	100	3	5	100	4	7	100	2	3	100
Fear Level												
Not at all High	7	12	12	8	13	13	7	12	12	2	3	3
Not High	16	27	38	16	27	40	25	42	53	18	30	33
High	20	33	72	22	37	77	17	28	82	23	38	72
Very High	13	22	93	11	18	95	7	12	93	15	25	97
No Response	4	7	100	3	5	100	4	7	100	2	3	100

Table 19 (Cont.)   *Summary of Frequencies and Percentages of the Scoring by Three Judges Regarding the Manifest Projective Content of Each of Four Stories for Outer-oriented Respondents and Inner-oriented Respondents.*

| | STORY 1 | | | | | | STORY 2 | | | | | |
| | Outer | | | Inner | | | Outer | | | Inner | | |
Judge 3	Freq	Adj %	Cum %	Freq	Adj %	Cum %	Freq	Adj %	Cum %	Freq	Adj %	Cum %
Thinking												
NNN	8	13	13	7	12	12	13	22	22	9	15	15
SNN	5	8	22	4	7	18	8	13	35	10	17	32
SNS	8	13	35	18	30	48	16	27	62	16	27	58
NNS	16	27	62	17	28	77	7	12	73	11	18	77
SSS	7	12	73	4	7	83	2	3	77	2	3	80
SSN	3	5	78	4	7	90	3	5	82	4	7	87
NSS	4	7	85	2	3	93	3	5	87	1	2	88
NSN	6	10	95	4	7	100	4	7	93	6	10	98
No Response	3	5	100				4	7	100	1	2	100
Feeling												
Mostly +	12	20	20	12	20	20	33	33	33	20	33	33
Mostly -	20	33	53	28	47	67	13	22	55	14	23	57
Mixed	24	40	93	19	32	98	21	35	90	22	37	93
Unclear	1	2	95	1	2	100	2	3	93	3	5	98
No Response	3	5	100				4	7	100	1	2	100
Doing												
Primarily CT	16	27	27	10	17	17	21	35	35	24	40	40
Primarily S	20	33	60	22	37	53	7	12	47	8	13	53
Primarily S/CT	13	22	82	16	27	80	13	22	68	9	15	68
Primarily CT/S	4	7	88	6	10	90	9	15	83	15	25	93
Unclear Movement	4	7	95	6	10	100	6	10	93	3	5	98
No Response	3	5	100				4	7	100	1	2	100
Outcome												
Came Together Positively	22	37	37	23	38	38	29	48	48	30	50	50
Came Together Negatively	6	10	47	3	5	43	7	12	60	5	8	58
Separated Positively	5	8	55	2	3	47	3	5	65	5	8	67
Separated Negatively	16	27	82	24	40	87	9	15	80	13	22	88
No Resolution	8	13	95	8	13	100	8	13	93	6	10	98
No Response	3	5	100				4	7	100	1	2	100
Fear Level												
Not at all High	5	8	8	5	8	8	13	22	22	8	13	13
Not High	20	33	42	12	20	28	14	23	45	15	25	38
High	23	38	80	34	57	85	22	37	82	28	47	85
Very High	9	15	95	9	15	100	7	12	93	8	13	98
No Response	3	5	100				4	7	100	1	2	100

Table 19 (Cont.)   Summary of Frequencies and Percentages of the Scoring by Three Judges Regarding the Manifest Projective Content of Each of Four Stories for Outer-oriented Respondents and Inner-oriented Respondents.

| | | STORY 3 | | | | | STORY 4 | | | | |
| | Outer | | | Inner | | | Outer | | | Inner | | |
Judge 3	Freq	Adj %	Cum %	Freq	Adj %	Cum %	Freq	Adj %	Cum %	Freq	Adj %	Cum %
Thinking												
NNN	8	13	13	8	13	13	7	12	12	4	7	7
SNN	4	7	20	2	3	17	1	2	13	2	3	10
SNS	11	18	38	18	30	47	4	7	20	4	7	17
NNS	27	45	83	21	35	82	2	3	23			
SSS	2	3	87	1	2	83				3	5	22
SSN				1	2	85	5	8	32	13	22	43
NSS	1	2	88	2	3	88	3	5	37	4	7	50
NSN	3	5	93	4	7	95	34	57	93	28	47	97
No Response	4	7	100	3	5	100	4	7	100	2	3	100
Feeling												
Mostly +	13	22	22	13	22	22	12	20	20	13	22	22
Mostly -	23	38	60	20	33	55	17	28	48	19	32	53
Mixed	20	33	93	21	35	90	26	43	92	26	43	97
Unclear				3	5	95	1	2	93			
No Response	4	7	100	3	5	100	4	7	100	2	3	100
Doing												
Primarily CT	16	27	27	8	13	13	22	37	37	27	45	45
Primarily S	17	28	55	15	25	38	2	3	40	3	5	50
Primarily S/CT	15	25	80	24	40	78	10	17	57	6	10	60
Primarily CT/S	6	10	90	5	8	87	8	13	70	12	20	80
Unclear Movement	2	3	93	5	8	95	14	23	93	10	17	97
No Response	4	7	100	3	5	100	4	7	100	2	3	100
Outcome												
Came Together Positively	24	40	40	24	40	40	28	47	47	28	47	47
Came Together Negatively	6	10	50	11	18	58	7	12	58	4	7	53
Separated Positively	2	3	53	2	3	62	5	8	67	4	7	60
Separated Negatively	16	27	80	13	22	83	5	8	75	8	13	73
No Resolution	8	13	93	7	12	95	11	18	93	14	23	97
No Response	4	7	100	3	5	100	4	7	100	2	3	100
Fear Level												
Not at all High	5	8	8	6	10	10	4	7	7	3	5	5
Not High	14	23	32	14	23	33	13	22	28	12	20	25
High	24	40	72	28	47	80	28	47	75	28	47	72
Very High	13	22	93	9	15	95	11	18	93	15	25	97
No Response	4	7	100	3	5	100	4	7	100	2	3	100

*Table 19 (Cont.)   Summary of Frequencies and Percentages of the Scoring
by Three Judges Regarding the Manifest Projective Content of Each of
Four Stories for Outer-oriented Respondents and Inner-oriented
Respondents.*

In the Table, NNN=No Inner Conflict/Tension, No External Conflict/Tension, No Conflict/Tension in the Relationship; SNN=Some Inner Conflict/Tension, No External Conflict/Tension, No Conflict/Tension in the Relationship; SNS=Some Inner Conflict/Tension, No External Conflict/Tension, Some Conflict/Tension in the Relationship; NNS=No Inner Conflict/Tension, No External Conflict/Tension, Some Conflict/Tension in the Relationship; SSS=Some Inner Conflict/Tension, Some External Conflict/Tension, Some Conflict/Tension in the Relationship; SSN=Some Inner Conflict/Tension, Some External Conflict/Tension, No Conflict/Tension in the Relationship; NSS=No Inner Conflict/Tension, Some External Conflict/Tension, Some Conflict/Tension in the Relationship; NSN=No Inner Conflict/Tension, Some External Conflict/Tension, No Conflict/Tension in the Relationship; CT=Coming Together; S=Separating; S/CT=Separating, followed by Coming Together; CT/S=Coming Together, followed by Separating.

respect to the degree of each), when intimacy without regard to race was an issue. Overall all three judges indicated that both Outer- and Inner-oriented respndents tended to depict (experience or project) a lesser amount of external conflict/tension when intimacy without regard to race was an issue.

With respect to the *Thinking* depicted for Story 3 (Black Boss of White Employees), all three judges indicated that both Outer- and Inner-oriented respondents primarily depicted (experienced or projected) more conflict/tension in the relationship itself when Black-White power relations was an issue. At least two judges also indicated that both groups tended to depict (experience or project) more internal than external conflict/tension in regard to Black-White power relations.

In terms of the *Thinking* depicted for Story 4 (Black-White Interracial Couple), all three judges indicated that both Outer- and Inner-oriented respondents depicted (experienced or projected) conflict/tension as external when Black-White interracial intimacy was an issue. The three judges varied in their assessment of the amount of internal conflict/tension vs. conflict/tension in the relationship itself, but at least two judges indicated that both groups tended to depict (experience or project) more internal conflict/tension than conflict/tension in the relationship itself when Black-White interracial intimacy was an issue.

Table 19 also demonstrates the *Affect (Feelings)* that was depicted in the four stories as each judge saw it for Outer- and Inner-oriented respondents. In terms of the *Affect* depicted for Story 1 (Boss of Employees), while the three judges varied a bit in their overall assessment of the *Affect* depicted by both groups, at least two judges indicated that both groups tended to depict (experience or project) primarily mixed and negative *Affects* when power without regard to race was an issue. At least two judges indicated that Outer-oriented respondents depicted (experienced or projected) more negative *Affect* than mixed *Affect* when power without regard to race was an issue.

In terms of the *Affect* depicted for Story 2 (Couple), though the three judges varied in their assessment of the degree of *Affect* depicted (experienced or projected), at least two judges generally indicated that Outer-oriented respondents depicted (experienced or projected) primarily positive and mixed affects, while the third judge saw them depicting (experiencing or projecting) primarily positive *Affect* when intimacy without regard to race was an issue. At least two judges indicated that Inner-oriented respondents depicted (experienced or projected) primarily mixed and positive *Affects*, while the third judge saw them depicting (experiencing or projecting) more positive than negative *Affect* when intimacy without regard to race was an issue.

In terms of the *Affect* depicted for Story 3 (Black Boss of White Employees), at least two judges indicated that Outer-oriented respondents overall depicted (experienced or projected) more negative *Affect*, with a tendency also to depict (experience or project) more mixed than positive *Affect*, when Black-White power relations was an issue. At least two judges indicated that Inner-oriented respondents depicted (experienced or projected) more mixed *Affect*, with a tendency also to depict (experience or project) more negative than positive *Affect* when Black-White power relations was an issue.

In terms of the *Affect* depicted for Story 4 (Black-White Interracial Couple), at least two judges indicated that both Outer- and Inner-oriented respondents depicted (experienced or projected) primarily mixed *Affect* when Black-White interracial intimacy was an issue. The judges varied in their assessment of how both groups depicted (experienced or projected) only positive *Affect* or only negative *Affect* when Black-White interracial intimacy was an issue.

Table 19 further illustrates the *Movement (or Doing)* (coming together vs separating) as each judge perceived it in the four stories. In terms of the *Movement* in Story 1 (Boss of Employees), at least two judges indicated that overall Outer-oriented respondents depicted (experienced or projected) the *Movement* as slightly more about coming together than about separating when power without regard to race was an issue. All three judges generally indicated, however, that overall Inner-oriented respondents depicted (experienced or projected) the *Movement* as more about separating than about coming together when power without regard to race was an issue.

With respect to the *Movement* depicted in Story 2 (Couple), all three judges indicated that both Outer- and Inner-oriented respondents depicted (experienced or projected) the *Movement* as mostly about coming together than about separating when intimacy without regard to race was an issue.

In terms of the *Movement* in Story 3 (Black Boss of White Employees), although the three judges varied slightly in their overall assessment of how Outer-oriented respondents depicted (experienced or projected) *Movement* in regard to Black-White power relations, at least two judges indicated that Outer-oriented respondnets tended to depict (experience or project) the *Movement* as slightly more about separating than about coming together when Black-White power relations was an issue. At least two judges indicated that Inner-oriented respondents depicted (experienced or projected) the *Movement* as more about coming together than about separating when Black-White power relations was an issue.

In terms of the *Movement* depicted in Story 4 (Black-White Interracial Couple), all three judges indicated that both Outer- and Inner-oriented respondents depicted (experienced or projected) the *Movement* as primarily about coming together when Black-White interracial intimacy was an issue.

The *Outcomes* regarding the four stories can also be seen in Table 19. In terms of *Outcomes* for Story 1 (Boss of Employees), all three judges indicated that Outer-oriented respondents resolved the conflict/tension more by having the characters to come together positively in the end when power without regard to race was an issue and at least two judges indicated that this was also true for Inner-oriented respondents.

In terms of *Outcomes* for Story 2 (Couple), all three judges indicated that both Outer- and Inner-oriented respondents resolved the conflict/tension primarily by having the characters to come together positively in the end when intimacy without regard to race was an issue.

In terms of *Outcomes* for Story 3 (Black Boss of White Employees), all three judges indicated that both Outer- and Inner-oriented respondents resolved the conflict/tension primarily by having the characters to come together positively in the end when Black-White power relations was an issue.

In terms of *Outcomes* for Story 4 (Black-White Interracial Couple), all three judges indicated that both Outer- and Inner-oriented respondents resolved the conflict/tension primarily by having the characters to come together positively in the end when Black-White interracial intimacy was an issue.

The judges also rated the Outer- and Inner-oriented respondents in terms of the *Level of Fear* in the manifest projective content of each story (see Table 19). For Story 1 (Boss of Employees), all three judges indicated that Inner-oriented respondents depicted (experienced or projected) more high Levels of Fear (though to varying degrees) than low and at least two judges indicated that Outer-oriented respondents also depicted (experienced or projected) more high Levels of Fear than low when power without regard to race was an issue.

For Story 2 (Couple), at least two judges indicated that Outer-oriented respondents depicted (experienced or projected) slightly more high *Levels of Fear* than low when intimacy without regard to race was an issue. All three judges indicated that Inner-oriented respondents depicted (experienced or projected) more high *Levels of Fear* than low when intimacy without regard to race was an issue.

For Story 3 (Black Boss of White Employees), all three judges indicated that Outer-oriented respondents depicted (experienced or projected) more high *Levels of Fear* than low when Black-White power relations was an issue. At least two judges indicated that Inner-oriented respondents depicted (experienced or projected) more high *Levels of Fear* than low when Black-White power relations was an issue.

For Story 4 (Black-White Interracial Couple), at least two judges indicated that Outer-oriented respondents depicted (experienced or projected) more low *Levels of Fear* than high when Black-White interracial intimacy was an issue. All three judges indicated that Inner-oriented respondents depicted more high *Levels of Fear* than low when Black-White interracial intimacy was an issue.

In sum, then, overall when power and intimacy were issues, without regard to race, both Outer- and Inner-oriented respondents tended to *Think* about conflicts/tensions in the "relationship itself," with a tendency also to manifest more "internal" than "external" conflict/tension. Further, while both groups tended to *Think* similarly in regard to Black-White power relations, each group tended to *Think* more about "external" conflict/tension in regard to Black-White interracial intimacy, with a tendency also to manifest more "internal" conflict/tension than conflict/tension in the "relationship itself." Basically, the "external" conflict/tension in regard to Black-White interracial intimacy was related to concern/anxiety about "what others think" and included such descriptions as "stares," "parental and/or family disapproval or alarm," "societal opposition or intolerance," and "public reactions." The *Thinking*, therefore, in regard to intimacy without regard to race vs Black-White interracial intimacy was significantly different for both Outer- and Inner-oriented respondents.

Overall, in terms of *Affect*, both groups manifested more mixed and/or negative feelings for the four projective situations. However, there was a significant difference between the two groups in relation to power without regard to race, as well as subtle differences between the two groups in relation to intimacy without regard to race and Black-White power relations. Positive *Affect* was also present for both groups in relation to intimacy without regard to race, but not in relation to Black-White interracial intimacy (primarily mixed affect here). Except for Outer-oriented respondents in regard to Black-White interracial intimacy, both groups tended to express more "High" than "Low" *Levels of Fear* in regard to the four projective situations. The findings here, then, provide some support for Hypothesis 3.

Overall, in terms of Movement, the two groups differed somewhat in expressing "separating vs coming together *Movement*" in relation to power, with and without regard to the Black race. That is, Inner-oriented respondents expressed more "separating" than "coming together" movement in relation to power without regard to race, while Outer-oriented respondents expressed this same kind of Movement more in relation to Black-White power relations. In the two intimacy situations, the two groups expressed the *Movement* as more about "coming together" than about "separating." To some extent, then, the findings provide additional support for Hypothesis 3.

Finally, both groups tended to resolve conflict or tension in regard to all four of the projective situations by having people come together in the end positively. So, despite all the *Thoughts* and *Feelings* in relation to the issues of power and intimacy, with and without regard to the Black Race, there appears to be a deep underlying desire for unity. If the Black Race represents the Unconscious self as contrasted with the Conscious self (the White Race), as suggested by the results of the factor analyses, the findings here may be indicating a strong desire to resolve the conflict/tension by seeing "the Self" as a "unified whole."

CONCLUSIONS

There were a number of significant findings in this exploratory study about the symbolic link between Anti-black disposition and Fear of (or Fear-related attributions), as well as Evaluative thoughts (or Evaluative attributions) about, the Nature of the Unconscious. Stimulated by Seth-Roberts' (1972) work, one implied assumption in the study was that the above link was supported or reinforced by the current color coding custom that involves the race-linked colors "black" and "white." That is, the color "black" by custom would carry more Fear-related and Negative qualities and be linked to "the Black Race" and "The Nature of the Unconscious" via similarities in affective meanings, particularly the quality "dark." The color "white" by custom would carry less Fear-related and more Positive qualities and be linked to "the White Race" and "The Nature of Consciousness" via similarities in affective meanings, particularly the quality "bright." Through these associative links, "the Black Race" may be representing or symbolizing the "Unconscious self," while "the White Race" may be representing the "Conscious self" for some Caucasians in American culture.

Hypothesis 1 of this study implied that a "black-Black Race-Unconscious" association and a "white-White Race-Consciousness" association would be more pronounced for Outer-oriented Caucasians than for Inner-oriented Caucasians and that the former association would be linked in semantic or "meaning space" to a subset of concepts such as "the Nature of" Satan, the Dreaming State, Death, and the Unknown, while the latter association would be linked in semantic or "meaning space" to a subset of concepts such as "the Nature of" God, the Waking State, and Life. Overall it was anticipated that the above associations and the other related concepts would be linked in semantic or "semantic space" together by Outer- and Inner-oriented Caucasians in somewhat different ways.

While overall clustering patterns that included all of the respective subsets of concepts did not occur in the exact manner predicted, some of the suggested links in semantic or "meanings space" among the concepts did occur. In fact, a major finding in the study was that a "black-Black Race-Unconscious" association and a "white-White Race-Consciousness" association were empirically demonstrated and that Outer- and Inner-oriented Caucasians dealt with these associations somewhat differently in regard to Fear and Evaluation, particularly in relation to the associative use of the race-linked colors black and white. For example, both of these associations were more pronounced for Outer-oriented Caucasians in an Evaluative context as they focused, respectively, on the issue of "The Nature of Death" and the color "white," while in the context of Fear, only a "black-Black Race" association was maintained and an association to the self-reference group (the White Race) emerged. For Inner-oriented Caucasians, however, the former association was more pronounced for them in the context of Fear, as they focused on "The Unknown," while evaluatively only a "Black Race-Unconscious" association was maintained without a significant link to the color "black." Further, only a "White Race-Consciousness" association was maintained by Inner-oriented Caucasians in both Fear and Evaluative contexts, without a significant link to the color "white." A few other concepts were also significantly associated with these patterns. The associative patterns that were found, then, tended to validate Hypothesis 1 of the study and to demonstrate the differential impact of an Outer vs Inner orientation on associative thought processes (or patterns of associative attributions).

The significance of the above findings is that they tended to support the idea that, for some Caucasians, the Black Race may represent the Unconscious self, while the White Race may represent the Conscious self and that Outer-oriented Caucasians may have a tendency to associatively use "both" the race-linked colors more so than Inner-oriented Caucasians in this regard (Seth-Roberts, 1972). The implication, therefore, of the empirically-derived "black-Black Race-Unconscious" association and the "white-White Race-Consciousness" association is that the scope of inquiry into the meaning of race and color should be broadened to include an investigation of attitudes about the "Inner life."

The literature suggested a link among color, race, and ideas about God and Satan (Bastide, 1970; Seth-Roberts, 1972). The overtones of religion, particularly the implication that people fear "the Nature of" God (or have fearful attributions associated with the God concept), were very much in evidence in the results of the factor analyses of this study. The findings tended to validate these associations, particularly the link between the religious concepts and the racelinked colors (i.e., the bipolar association of "white-God" and "black-Satan"). Associatively, the concept of God tended to emerge more often for Outer-oriented Caucasians than for Inner-oriented Caucasians. This was consistent with another finding in the study, which indicated that Outer-oriented Caucasians tended to go to church more often than Inner-oriented Caucasians.

One interesting implication of the above findings, as farfetched as it may sound on the surface, is that one step in helping to resolve Black-White Race problems in American culture may be for individuals to examine their current ideas or concepts about "The Nature of God and Satan." That is, what some Caucasians may be really dealing with is the power of their own projections of Fear and Evaluative thoughts (or fearful and evaluative attributions) about the "Inner self," and these projections may have become associated with their current ideas about "the Nature of" God, Satan, the Black Race, the White Race, Life, Death, the Waking State, the Dreaming State, Consciousness, the Unconscious, the Unknown and the colors black and white in terms of Fear and Evaluative judgments. The purpose here is not to argue the validity of God or the God concept, but rather to argue that there may be certain distortions in regard to conceptualizations or ideas about "the Nature of" God and these distortions may be significantly impacting on the human experience of the races. Another illustration is provided by the many wars that have been and are currently being fought in the name of religion, as each group defends what it perceives to be the "correct" view about God and reality (i.e., Crusades; Catholics and Protestants in Northern Ireland; Jews and Palestinians or Arab Muslims in the Middle East; Iran and Iraq).

Allport (1954) suggested that the major problem in prejudice is, in fact, a thought problem. A number of independent "associative thought patterns" or "patterns of associative attributions," each with a particular "priority focus" (highest loading item on a Factor), were found in this study for Outer-oriented and Inner-oriented Caucasians in regard to Fear and Evaluation. For each group, it can be argued that the priority foci for the various Factors constitute "core concepts" that may emerge and interact in an interracial context, along with their associative thought patterns or patterns of associative attributions, to target the Black Race for anti-black prejudice. For example, the findings in regard to a "Death-Black Race-Unconscious" association may be illustrating how Outer- and Inner-oriented Caucasians may differentially link in the "cultural meaning space" the Black Race to their perceptions of "the Natue of" Death as the annihilation of Consciousness. Seth-Roberts (1972) argued that a person's ideas about light and darkness and God and Satan are involved here. That is, Life and Death tend to be viewed in terms of black and white and the value judgments of good and evil–the annihilation of Consciousness being perceived as black and its resurrection as white. Further, there was some support for William's (1973) theory of a link between Anti-black Disopositions and earlier learned attitudes about light (the Waking State/day) and darkness (the Dreaming State/night). The findings here, however, go one step further in terms of linking either "the Nature of" the Waking State or the Dreaming State to race, Consciousness, and/or the Unconscious, depending on the priority focus, the person's Outer or Inner orientation, and the context (Fear or Evaluative) in which the concepts were being considered.

The findings in regard to priority foci and "associative thought processes" or "patterns of associative attributions" may have implications for understanding Anti-black Dispositions in terms of the three cognitive processes extensively studied by Tajfel and his associates (1963, 1964, 1969, 1970, 1974). That is, in an interracial context involving Fear or Evaluative judgments, the "core concepts" may serve as seeds for the cognitive processes of "categorization" (the making of social categories), "assimilation" (learning social values and norms to provide content for the social categories), and "search for coherence" (making attributions based on the social categories and what has been learned) (Tajfel, 1969). These processes, then, in accord with the priority foci and "associative thought patterns" or "patterns of associative attributions" found in this study, may help to structure and give meaning to the reality of some Caucasians with anti-black attitudes. The findings suggest that an Outer vs Inner orientation may differentially influence these processes in terms of determining the priority focus, modifying the salience of certain concepts, or masking the general associative links among the concepts.

It was implied in the study that a "black-Black Race-Unconscious" association, along with a subset of concepts such as "the Nature of" Satan, the Dreaming State, Death, and the Unknown would have similar affective meanings and that a "white-White Race-Consciousness" association, along with a subset of concepts such as "the Nature of" God, the Waking State, and Life would have similar affective meanings. That is, the former subset of concepts would be evaluated more negatively, while the latter subset of concepts would be evaluated more positively in "meaning space." The assumption here is that these respective subsets of concepts would have more in common with the respective race-linked colors black and white than vice versa. It was also anticipated that overall Outer- and Inner-oriented Caucasians would deal with these various concepts (rate them on a Semantic Differential or SD) in somewhat different ways in terms of affective meanings that are given to the concepts.

In general, the findings tended to support the above ideas (Hypotheses 1-a and 1-b). That is, overall the former subset of concepts above did tend to have specific affective qualities (affective meanings) more in common with the color "black" and overall the latter subset of concepts above did tend to have specific affective qualities (affective meanings) more in common with the color "white." This was true particularly in regard to the "dark-bright" quality, the "bad-good" quality and the "primitive-civilized" quality. While these tendencies were found for both Outer- and Inner-oriented Caucasians, they tended to occur slightly more for Outer-oriented Caucasians than for Inner-oriented Caucasians (e.g., except for "The Nature of the Unconscious/me," the SD ratings by Outer-oriented Caucasians, but not for as many concepts by Inner-oriented Caucasians indicated that the "dark" quality or a rating closer to the dark quality tended to occur for all stimulus items in the former subset of concepts and a "brighter" quality for all stiumulus items in the latter subset of concepts). Further, the SD ratings indicated that the color "black" had more "High Fear" qualities and was more "Negative," while the color "white" had more "Low Fear" qualities and was "Positive." Overall, the SD ratings by Outer-oriented Caucasians indicated that the color "black" had somewhat less Understandability and that the color "white" was significantly more "Potent" to them than the ratings by Inner-oriented Caucasians.

In accord with the race-linked colors, then, the SD ratings by Outer-oriented Caucasians and Inner-oriented Caucasians indicated that the two groups tended to respond differentially to "The Black Race" and "The White Race" concepts in terms of affective meanings. That is, in regard to "The Black Race, the SD ratings by Outer-oriented Caucasians overall tended to lean more in a "Negative" direction with some "High Fear" qualities involved, while the SD ratings by Inner-oriented Caucasians overall tended to lean more in a "Positive" direction with some "High Fear" qualities involved. In contrast, the SD ratings by Outer-oriented Caucasians indicated that "The White Race" concept overall was significantly more "Positive" and had somewhat higher Understandability to them than the ratings by Inner-oriented Caucasiand. The "dark-bright" quality also appeared to be somewhat more pronounced for Outer-oriented Caucasians, but not as much for Inner-oriented Caucasians in regard to the race names. In fact, for Outer-oriented Caucasians but not as intensely for Inner-oriented Caucasians, one of the *common qualities* or *affective meanings* for a "black-Black Race-Unconscious" association was at least a "Tendency Toward dark" or a SD rating closer to this tendency. For both Outer- and Inner-oriented Caucasians, one of the *common qualities* or *affective meanings* for a "white-White Race-Consciousness" association was the quality "bright." These findings are consistent with the results of the factor analyses and tend to support Seth-Roberts' (1972) premise in regard to the "darkbright" quality. The "dark-bright" quality appears indeed to be a significant consideration in the meaning of race and color in American culture, at least as indicated by the respondents in this study.

In general, then, it was found that, in many instances, Outer-oriented Caucasians and Inner-oriented Caucasians did deal with the various concepts (rated them on the SD) in significantly different ways in terms of "meaning space." The dimension, however, on which the concept was being considered, was important. That is, on some dimensions, there may have been an overall neutral response, but when specific qualities or affective meanings (dark vs bright) on a given dimension (i.e., Fear, Evaluative, etc.) were examined, there may have been significant differences in the respective responses of the two groups. Further, while both groups may have had similar overall responses on a given dimension or in reference to a given quality or affective meaning, there were significant differences between the two groups in terms of the relative intensity of their responses.

Seth-Roberts (1972) argued that "we create our own realities according to the nature of our beliefs." The findings in regard to affective meanings for the concepts in this study may be illustrating how Outer- and Inner-oriented Caucasians give differential racial meaning to the self, not-self, and their respective worlds. The findings elaborate on Williams' (1964, 1974, 1976) earlier studies in regard to color connotations and race names, but they also go a step further in linking connotatively the respective religious concepts and concepts about "the Nature of" Consciousness, the Unconscious, the Dreaming State, the Waking State, Life, Death, and the Unknown as Outer- and Inner-oriented Caucasians may differentially use them. There was also support in these findings for Allport's (1954) "strangeness" hypothesis (i.e., fear of the strange) in terms of how Outer-oriented Caucasians gave meaning to "The Black Race" concept. The SD ratings by both groups, however, indicated that the color black, the Unconscious, Satan, the Dreaming State, Death, and the Unknown were all "strange" to them.

The affective meanings that are reflected in this study for the various concepts, appear to be indicating deeply ingrained cultural fears (or fearful attributions) and evaluative attitudes about the meaning of race, color, the Conscious self, and the Unconscious self in American culture. Only preliminary evidence exists for the fear-threat syndrome in regard to Black-White relations (Maykovitch, 1972; Groves & Rossi, 1970), but these findings suggest that more research in regard to the Fear component would be enlightening. Numerous studies have attempted to determine how evaluative attitudes (meanings) about the Black Race are acquired. Some of the notions include (1) direct instruction (Harris, Cough, & Martin, 1950; Radke-Yarrow, Trager, & Miller, i952; Liebert, Sobol, & Copemann, 1972), (2) reinforcement (Williams & Roberson, 1967; Williams, Tucker, & Dunham, 1971; Doke & Risley, 1972; Katz, Henchy, & Allen, 1968), (3) personality factors and child-rearing techniques (Adorno, Frenkel-Brunswick, Levinson, & Sanford, 1950; Harris et al., 1950; Epstein & Komorita, 1965), (4) cognitive aspects of racial attitudes (Frenkel-Brunswick, 1948; Kutner, 1958; Tajfel, 1973), and (5) perceptual factors (Allport, 1954; Cantor, 1972; Katz & Zalk, 1974; Katz & Seavey, 1973).

Goodman (1964) has suggested a three-stage theory of racial attitude development, consisting of ethnic awareness (ages 3-4), ethnic orientation (4-7), and then attitudes. Katz (1976), however, in an attempt to synthesize the many findings, has suggested at least eight overlapping, but separable, steps in the developmental sequence of racial attitude acquisition, which spans approximately the first 10 years of the person's life. These steps include (1) early observation of racial cues, (2) formation of rudimentary concepts, (3) conceptual differentiation, (4) recognition of the irrevocability of cues, (5) consolidation of group concepts, (6) perceptual elaboration, (7) cognitive elaboration, and (8) attitude crystallization. What the findings in this study in regard to affective meanings add is a link to the meanings given to "Conscious self" and "Unconscious self" as the above evaluative attitudinal developments are taking place and how an Outer vs Inner orientation may differentially affect these meanings.

One implication of the findings in regard to affective meanings is that there seems to be a need to reformulate ideas and connotations about the color "black" and "The Nature of the Unconscious" in order to modify the conscious experience that some Caucasians, at least as revealed in this study, may have in relation to the Black Race. That is, the findings regarding the affective meanings for the various concepts for Outer- and Inner-oriented Caucasians seem to be reflecting some deeply ingrained cultural fears (or fear-related attributions) and evaluative orientations to which some Caucasian individuals are exposed in developing a sense of self, not self, and the world. These cultural fears (or fear-related attributions) and evaluative orientations, then, need to be examined.

The literature suggests that one characteristic of an Outer-oriented person is that the person tends to reject emotions or tends to be more reserved in their emotional expression (Murray, 1938; Sanford et al., 1950). In this light, it was anticipated in this study that Outer-oriented Caucasians would "indicate" a lower Level of Fear than Inner-oriented Caucasians when these respective groups were engaged in induced projective activities such as story writing and expressing an attitude about an object (attitude-confrontation). However, when the Black Race is a factor, the expectation was that the Level of Fear would increase for both groups.

The findings in this study, in part, supported the general thrust of the above notions (Hypothesis 2). That is, it was found that Outer-oriented Caucasians indicated significantly lower Levels of Fear than Inner-oriented Caucasians *After* the writing of each of four Projective Stories. One implication of this finding is that Inner-oriented Caucasians were more willing to reflect on their feelings *After* the experience of writing each of the Projective Stories, whereas Outer-oriented Caucasians tended to reject their emotions. This interpretation was consistent with other findings in the study in terms of how each group tended to describe itself (i.e., Inner-oriented Caucasians as "Feeling Types" and Outer-oriented Caucasians as "Thinking Types"), how each group tended to "indicate" their respective state anxiety (i.e., Outer-oriented Caucasians tended to indicate a lower state anxiety), how Murray (1938) characterized an Inner-(Intraceptive) vs an Outer-(Extraceptive) oriented person (i.e., an Extraceptive person tends to be afraid of genuine feelings because they might get out of control), and how three judges tended to evaluate the Level of Fear in the content of the Projective Stories (i.e., more "high" than "low").

It was also found that there was a significant effect of the person's Outer vs Inner orientation in regard to a change in Level of Fear from *Before* to *After* when dealing with power without regard to race. That is, the two groups differed significantly from each other in terms of a change in level of fear from *Before* to *After* as a result of dealing with the issue of power without regard to race.

In terms of general patterns of increase (*Before* vs *During*), decrease (*During* vs *After*), and change (*Before* vs *After*) in level of fear for each group, respectively, a number of significant findings occurred. For Outer-oriented Caucasians, the Level of Fear increased significantly when dealing with Black-White power relations, Black-White interracial intimacy, and intimacy without regard to race, decreased significantly from *During* to *After* for all four projective situations, and changed significantly when dealing with power without regard to race (lower *After* than *Before*) and when dealing with intimacy without regard to race (higher *After* than *Before*). For Inner-oriented Caucasians, when dealing with power and intimacy, with and without regard to the Black Race (all four projective situations), the Level of Fear increased significantly from *Before* to *During*, decreased significantly from *During* to *After*, but overall did not change significantly from *Before* to *After* as a result of the experience of writing the stories. For both Outer- and Inner-oriented Caucasians, the findings indicated that the Level of Fear *After* dealing with Black-White power relations was significantly higher than the Level of Fear *After* dealing with power without regard to race. Overall it was found that both groups tended to approach life in a fairly fearful way (i.e., there was somewhat high general trait anxiety for both groups). When the Black Race is made salient, however, it does appear to have impact on the person's experience of Fear, particularly in regard to the issue of Black-White power relations *After* the fact. Outer-oriented Caucasians appear also to use some denial in this regard.

In regard to the projective experience of expressing attitudes about the Black Race (i.e., Multifactor Racial Attitude Inventory experience or MRAI experience), the findings indicated that for both Outer- and Inner-oriented Caucasians, the Level of Fear increased significantly from *Before* to *During* the experience, decreased significantly from *During* to *After*, but did not change significantly from *Before* to *After* the experience of expressing attitudes about the Black race. While there were no significant differences between the two groups in regard to this experience, the Level of Fear indicated by Outer-oriented Caucasians was actually slightly higher than the Level of Fear indicated by Inner-oriented Caucasians *Before* the MRAI experience, slightly lower than the Level of Fear indicated by Inner-oriented Caucasians *During* the MRAI experience, and actually dropped slightly lower than the Level of Fear indicated by Inner-oriented Caucasians *After* the MRAI experience. A general impression, then, in accord with Hypothesis 2 of the study, was that Outer-oriented Caucasians tended to reject their emotions *During* the MRAI experience and appeared to be somewhat more relieved *After* the MRAI experience.

The findings in regard to induced projection and level of fear have implications for the contact hypothesis (Mann, 1959; Cook, 1962; Minard, 1952; Sherif, 1966). The contact hypothesis simply states that contact between people–the mere fact of interaction–is likely to change their beliefs and feelings toward each other. Amir (1969) reviewed the status of the contact hypothesis and noted certain conditions to reduce prejudice. Cook (1970) in a study created five conditions: (1) equal status contact between Blacks and Whites, (2) a favorable social climate for intergroup contact, (3) intimate rather than casual contact, (4) pleasant and rewarding contact, and(5) the members in both groups engage in an activity with a mutual superordinate goal. The findings in this study, then, add a perspective about the issue of "projectivity" and Fear in terms of how Outer- and Inner-oriented Caucasians may deal with interracial contacts involving the issues of power and intimacy. That is, when contact occurs, "projection" may take place and the person's Level of Fear may increase, decrease, or change as indicated by the findings. Further, the findings in regard to attitude-confrontation may have relevance for Rokeach's (1971) work in regard to the effects of exposing states of inconsistency.

In regard to attitudes about the Black Race, a major finding in this study was that Outer- and Inner-oriented Caucasians had significantly different attitudes towards the Black Race in many instances. More specifically, it was found that Outer-oriented Caucasians had significantly more of an Anti-black Disposition than Inner-oriented Caucasians in terms of attitudes about the use of Segregation-Integration Policies to address inequities between the races, the Inferiority of the Black Race, Ease in Interracial Contact with the Black Race, the use of the idea of Private Rights to avoid addressing inequities between the races, and the use of the idea of Gradualism to avoid addressing inequities between the races. There was also a tendency for Inner-oriented Caucasians to be less anti-black in their disposition on all of the attitude dimensions that were measured on a Multifactor Racial Attitude Inventory. Overall, the highest Anti-black Disposition tended to occur for both groups in regard to "Ease in Interracial Contact" and "Gradualism." The use of "Gradualism" in regard to ideas about change has been studied as one form of symbolic racism (Sears and Kinder, 1970). These findings, then, validated part of Hypothesis 3, which predicted that there would be a difference between Outer- and Inner-oriented Caucasians in regard to Anti-black Disposition and specifically in regard to the kind of attitudes each group had toward the Black Race.

In terms of an evaluation of the content of the projective stories in this study, the findings indicated that *Thinking* in regard to intimacy without regard to race vs Black-White interracial intimacy was significantly different for both Outer- and Inner-oriented Caucasians. That is, in the latter situation, both groups *thought* more about "external" conflict/tension, characterized by "what others think." These included anxieties/concerns about other people staring, parental and/or family dispproval or alarm, societal opposition or intolerance, and public reactions/insensitivity.

In terms of *Affect*, there was a significant difference between the two groups in terms of *Feelings* manifested in regard to power without regard to race. Overall, however, both groups tended to manifest more mixed and/or negative feelings for the four projective stories, with some positive feelings only in regard to the issue of intimacy without regard to race. Except for Outer-oriented Caucasians in regard to Black-White interracial intimacy, both groups tended to express more "High" than "Low" *Levels of Fear* in regard to four Projective Stories. Some support for Hypothesis 3 is provided by these findings.

In terms of *Movement*, Inner-oriented Caucasians expressed more "separating" than "coming together" movement in relation to power without regard to race, while Outer-oriented Caucasians expressed this same kind of movement in relation to Black-White power relations. The two groups expressed more "coming together" than "separating" movement in regard to the two intimacy situations. To some extent, these findings also tend to support Hypothesis 3.

Lastly, both groups tended to resolve conflict or tension in regard to all four projective situations by having people come together positively in the end. The implication is that despite all the *Thoughts* and *Feelings* in relation to power and intimacy, with and without regard to the Black Race, there appears to be a deep underlying desire for unity. The significance of this finding, then, is that if the Black Race represents the "Unconscious self" as contrasted with the "Conscious self" (the White Race), as suggested by the results of the factor analyses, there may be a strong desire to resolve the conflict/tension by seeing "the Self" as a "unified whole."

The White Race and the Black Race as concepts in the "cultural meaning space" seem very much linked in the psyche for the Caucasians respondents in this study and perhaps for many Caucasians in the United States. Many of the findings argue for a need to examine ideas and beliefs in order to gain more self-insight and accept the "whole self." It has been demonstrated that self-insight reduces prejudice (Stotland, Katz, & Patchen, 1959). It has also been demonstrated that there is a correlation between negative self-attitudes and rejection of others (Ehrlich, 1973, pp. 131–133), a negative correlation between self-esteem and anti-black prejudice (Rubin, 1967), and a relationship between self-identity and religion (Bastide, 1976). Further, it has been found that as acceptance of self increases, acceptance of others also increases (Weissbach, 1976). Accepting the "Whole self," which also implies accepting one's own "Inner self," may lead to a further reduction of the need to symbolically link the Black Race with Fears (or Fear-related attributions) and Evaluative thoughts (or Evaluative attributions) about this "Inner life."

The findings in this study tend to support the idea that an Inner orientation tends to be more characteristic of the unprejudiced (Adorno et al., 1950). In the study, it was first established that Outer- and Inner-oriented Caucasians did differ significantly from one another. Murray's (1938) characterization of these orientations as differences in attitudes about "the Nature of" the Inner life was evident in that Outer-oriented Caucasians tended to describe themselves more as "Thinking Types" than as "Feeling Types," while Inner-oriented Caucasians tended to describe themselves more as "Feeling Types" than as "Thinking Types." While similar to each other in many respects, subtle differences were found between Outer- and Inner-oriented Caucasians in terms of the importance that each group attached to intuition and hunches, the tendency to remember their dreams, the nature of their dreams, their respective openness, their church-going habits, their indicated state anxiety, their other-race contact, and the nature of their other-race contact. While not specifically related to the main hypotheses of the study, these findings may help to explain the differential experience that Outer- vs Inner-oriented Caucasians may have in relation to the Black Race. That is, these findings further support the idea that there is some connection between Outer vs Inner orientations and how these different orientations (even as subtle in character as differentiated in this study) may impact on the expression of religion and race contact.

Interestingly, however, both Outer- and Inner-oriented Caucasians identified themselves more by using only race (primarily) or only ethnic labels (as opposed to both) when asked to identify themselves by "Race and/or Ethnicity" (there were also race and nationality responses, etc.). This finding suggests that despite the Outer vs Inner orientation, race or ethnic labeling was a salient issue for the Caucasians respondents in this study and perhaps in this country. The importance of including these findings is that they may be illustrating a cultural norm for some Caucasians which impacts on how they think about the issue of race and which apparently overshadows the person's Outer vs Inner orientation. A number of studies have indicated that race and ethnic labeling may facilitate discrimination between groups, but that it also blinds and reduces the capacity for differentiating among individual members (Katz, 1973; Katz & Zalk, 1974; Katz, Sohn, & Zalk, 1974; Katz & Seavey, 1973). This finding, then, supports the many theorists and other findings which indicate that in this country the development of racial and ethnic attitudes is integrally related to the establishment of a child's self-identity which carries over into adult life (Goodman, 1952; Proshansky, 1966; Porter, 1971). The result is that ideas about the "Conscious self" are also formed and reinforced in this context, which may then impact on race relations.

When Ethnocentricism and Underlying Feeling States were specifically examined in this study, no significant differences were found between Outer- and Inner-oriented Caucasians in terms of their Ethnocentrism, with some slight variations regarding Underlying Feeling States. A significant difference between the two groups had been hypothesized. An interesting, unexpected finding, however, was that "Moods" for the Caucasian respondents generally tended to generate a "Low" Ethnocentric orientation (responses), while things that "Drive People Nuts" generally tended to generate a "High" Ethnocentric orientation (responses), irrespective of a person's Outer or Inner orientation. This finding may be added to the already existing evidence of a correlation between various indices of self-reported dissatisfaction with one's condition in life (which presumably indicates "free-floating aggression" due to frustration) and ethnic prejudice (Gordon, 1943; Allport & Kramer, 1946; Campbell, 1947; Rosenblith, 1949).

So, while an Inner orientation does appear to be facilitative in regard to race relations, there continue to be problems for some Caucasians in this country in regard to race and color. Pinderhughes (1971) and Wadeson (1971) offered different projection theories of white racism. The first is based on self-hatred, while in the second, projection serves to maintain in-group solidarity. The findings in this exploratory study of the symbolic link between Anti-black Dispositions toward the Black Race and the Unconscious suggest that projection may mediate or act as a vehicle of expression for a "black-Black Race-Unconscious" association and a "white-White Race-Consciousness" association. Seth-Roberts (1972) argues that we see what we want to see and that this is in accord with our thoughts and emotional attitudes about physical reality.

In terms of everyday reality, the symbolism contained in American culture tends to affirm the associative thought patterns (or patterns of associative attributions) and connotations revealed for the various concepts in this study. For example, the portrayal in the media of urban Black life as a ghetto filled with crime, supported by linguistic symbolism, may affirms for some Caucasians that the Black Race represents the underside of the "proper American citizen," while they represent the "conscious and objective," more proper side of the self. Ideas about good and evil, right and wrong may tend to emerge here, as religious icons reinforce the image of a "white God" with which Caucasians in American culture can easily identify. What is ignored by this portrayal is the reality that the vast majority of African Americans (or people of African descent) who live in these areas are not involved in any crimes and are decent, hard-working people struggling to survive.

It can be argued, therefore, that as race, religion, or status issues become salient for some Caucasians in everyday reality in American society, particularly for Outer-oriented Caucasians, the "associative thought patterns" (or patterns of associative attributions) found in this study, supported by the often negative portrayal of African Americans (or the Black Race) in the media and elsewhere, may get activated and reinforced as individuals focus on examples of the most extreme members. The connotations that were found in this study in regard to race names, color, religious concepts, Day and Night, Life and Death, Consciousness and the Unconscious, and the Unknown may also get activated and reinforced. One impact appears to be on the person's daily considerations about "the Conscious self" and "Unconscious self." Furthermore, what the study reveals is that Fear (or Fear-related attributions) and Evaluative thoughts (or Evaluative attributions) about "The Nature of the Unconscious" are very salient considerations for some Caucasians, irrespective of an Outer or Inner orientation, and that an Outer orientation tends to enhance the salience for considerations about "The Nature of Consciousness."

As stated earlier, the present study should be regarded as a first step in an exploratory process. There are a number of possibilities for future research. For example, since this study focused solely on Caucasians, a comparative study involving both African American and Caucasian American respondents would provide a cross-racial perspective. Such a study may reveal differences with regard to associative thought patterns (or patterns of associative attributions) and connotations for the various concepts between African Americans and Caucasian Americans. William Cross' (1972) work in regard to a process of discovering what he calls the "black referrent" (quest for a black identity) would have relevance for such a sudy. That is, he describes a five stage process, propelled by black rage, guilt, pride, and self-examination of beliefs, whereby a black person moves from a world view dominated by Euro-American determinants to a world view that supercedes either/or paradigms of thought. He labeled the stages (1) pre-encounter (a person thinks, acts, and behaves in a manner that degrades blackness), (2) encounter (a verbal or visual event that causes a person to begin to reinterpret the world), (3) immersion-emersion (a person immerses him/herself in the world of blackness by turning inward and withdrawing from everything that represents the white world; the white world is dehumanized; s/he then emerges from the deadend, either/or oversimplified way of thinking with awareness and a sense of control of his/her experiences; whites are rehumanized), (4) internalization (a person achieves a feeling of inner security and is satisfied with him/herself), and (5) internalization-commitment (a person becomes committed to a plan or vision for expressing the self, which affirms all of what the person is). This author would hasten to add that what really gets discovered is what the person's own "blackness" means to him/herself, apart from the projections that others might have about him/her.

In accord with the above stages, it would be anticipated in a cross-racial study that a black person in stage one would tend to be more Outer-oriented and hence could tend to exhibit similar "associative thought patterns" (or pattens of associative attributions) and connotations in regard to the various concepts as Outer-oriented Caucasians. There may also be different associative thought patterns (or patterns of associative attributions) and connotative responses that emerge for each of the subsequent stages. A black person in stage three might in fact invert the whole associative process or pattern of associations. Also, a flexibility variable in regard to an Outer-Inner orientation might be an important variable. That is, the person's ability to comfortably deal with both outer and inner content may be more reflective of an unprejudiced orientation than a highly Inner orientation per se. A cross-racial study would allow for such an hypothesis to be tested for both groups.

The above considerations in regard to the idea of flexibility could also be extended to a multicultural study. A multicultural study would provide, moreover, a perspective about the universality or generalizability of the findings in this study. Though Williams (1973) has demonstrated that many cultures prefer light to dark colors, Western and non-Western cultures tend to deal with the "Inner life" somewhat differently. That is, Western cultures tend to be more mechanistic and materialistic (Outer-oriented), while non-Western cultures (Eastern and African) tend to legitimize aspects of the inner world more so through certain customs, practices, and rituals. While it would be anticipated in a multicultural study that projection (implying fear of or fearful attributions about the unconscious) and "associative thought patterns" (or patterns of associative attributions) would be found in regard to an out-group, the specific connotative qualities that may be applied toward the out-group may vary from culture to culture. If the Black Race is an identified out-group in the particular culture (currently or historically), it is anticipated that findings similar to those obtained in the present study would result (i.e., South Africa).

This study, for the most part, supports the premise that the Black Race may have come to represent the "Unconscious self" as contrasted with the "Conscious self" for some Caucasians in American culture. Cultural fears (or Fear-related attributions) and Evaluative orientations, particularly in regard to the race-linked colors, appear to support or reinforce these associations. The findings in this study suggest that race reality continues to be perceived in a distorted manner and that there is a need to examine "associative thought patterns" (or patterns of associative attributions) and connotations in regard to the meaning of race, color, and the nature of the unconscious.

REFERENCES

Adler, A. (1956) *The Individual Psychology of Alfred Adler: A Systematic Presentation in Selections from His Writings.* H.L. Ansbacher & R.R. Ansbacher (Eds.). New York, NY: Harper.

Adorno, T.W., Frenkel-Brunswik, E., Levinson, D., & Sanford, R.N. (1950) *The Authoritarian Personality.* New York, NY: W.W. Norton.

Akutagawa, D.A. (1956) A study in construct validity of the psychoanalytic concept of latent anxiety and a test of projection distance hypotheses. Unpublished doctoral dissertation, University of Pittsburgh.

Allport, G.W., & Kramer, B.M. (1946) Some roots of prejudice. *Journal of Psychology,* (22), 9-39.

Allport, G.W. (1954) *The Nature of Prejudice.* Cambridge, MA: Addison-Wesley.

Amir, Y. (1969) Contact hypothesis in ethnic relations. *Psychological Bulletin,* (71), 319-342.

Ashmore, R.D., & Del Boca, F.K. (1976) Psychological approaches to understanding intergroup conflict. In P.A. Katz (Ed.), *Toward the Elimination of Racism.* New York, NY: Pergamon Press.

Bastide, R. (1970) Color, racism, and Christianity. In B.N. Schwartz & R. Disch (Eds.), *White Racism–Its History, Pathology, and Practice.* New York, NY: Dell Publishing Co.

Billig, M.G., & Tajfel, H. (1973) Social categorization and similarity in intergroup behavior. *European Journal of Social Psychology,* (3), 27-52.

Blake, R., & Dennis, W. (1943) The development of stereotypes concerning the
    Negro. *Journal of Abnormal and Social Psychology,* (38), 525-531.

Block, J. (1957) Studies in the phenomenology of emotions. *Journal of Abnormal
    and Social Psychology,* 54, 358-363.

Campbell, A.A. (1947) Factors associated with attitudes toward Jews. In T.M.
    Newcomb & E.L. Hartley (Eds.), *Reading in Social Psychology.* New
    York, NY: Bolt.

Cantor, G.N. (1972) Effects of familiarization on children's ratings of pictures of
    whites and blacks. *Child Development,* (43), 12191229.

Cook, S.W. (1962) The systematic analysis of socially significant events: a
    strategy for social research. *Journal of Social Issues,* 18(2), 66-84.

Cook, S.W. (1970) The effects of unintended interracial contact upon racial
    interaction and attitude change. Final report, August, 1970. University of
    Colorado. Contract OEC

Cross, W. (1972) Toward a psychology of Black liberation. In C. Young (Ed.),
    Black Experience–Analysis and Synthesis. San Rafael, CA: Leswing
    Press.

Dickson, C.R. (1975) Role of assessment in behavior therapy. In P. McReynolds
    (Ed.), *Advances in Psychological Assessment III.* San Francisco, CA:
    Jossey-Bass.

Doke, L.A., & Risley, T.R. (1972) Some discriminative properties of race and sex
    for children from an all-Negro neighborhood. *Child Development,* (43),
    677-681.

Donnerstein, E., Simon, S., & Ditrichs, R. (1972) Variables in interracial aggression: Anonymity, expected retaliation, and a riot. *Journal of Personality and Social Psychology*, (22), 236-245.

Drake, St. Clair. (1972) The black experience in black historical perspective. In C. Young (Ed.), *Black Experience–Analysis and Synthesis*. San Rafael, CA: Leswing Press.

Ehrlich, H.J. (1973) *The Social Psychology of Prejudice*. New York, NY: Wiley.

Epstein, R., & Komorita, S.S. (1965) Parental discipline, stimulus characteristics of outgroups, and social distance in children. *Journal of Personality and Social Psychology*, (2), 416-420.

Fagan, J.F. (1974) Infant color perception. *Science*, (183), 973-975.

Frenkel-Brunswik, E. (1948) A study of prejudice in children. *Human Relations*, (1), 295-306.

Freud, S. (1916) The unconscious. In J. Strachey, A. Freud, A. Strachey, & A. Tyson (Eds.), *The Standard Edition of the Complete Psychological Works of Sigmund Freud*, (14), 161-215. London: Hogarth Press.

Geer, J.H. (1965) The development of a scale to measure fear. *Behavior Research Therapy*, (3), 45-53.

Gergen, (1967) The significance of skin color in human relations. *Daedalus*, 390-406.

Goldschmid, M.L. (Ed.) (1970) *Black Americans and White Racism*. New York: Holt, Rinehart, and Winston.

Goodman, M.E. (1964) *Race Awareness In Young Children*. New York, NY: Collier Books, 1964.

Gordon, A.I. (1943) Frustration and aggression among Jewish university students. *Jewish Sociological Studies*, (5), 27-42.

Groves, W.E., & Rossi, P.H. (1970) Police perceptions of a hostile ghetto realism or projection. *American Behavioral Scientist*, 13, 727-744.

Halsey, M. (1946) *Color Blind*. New York, NY: Simon & Schuster.

Harris, D., Cough, H., & Martin, W.E. (1950) Children's ethnic attitudes. II: relationships to parental beliefs concerning child training. *Child Development*, (21), 169-181.

Hershenson, M. (1964) Visual discrimination in the human newborn. *Journal of Comparative and Physiological Psvchology*, 58(2), 270-276.

Homey, K. (1939) *New Ways in Psychoanalysis*. New York, NY: W.W. Norton.

Homey, K. (1945) *Our Inner Conflicts*. New York, NY: W.W. Norton.

Horowitz, R.E. (1939) Racial aspects of self-identification in nursery school children. *Journal of Psychology*, (7), 91-99.

Isaacs, H.R. (1963) *The New World of Negro Americans*. New York, NY: John Day.

Jordan, W.D. (1968) *White Over Black: American Attitudes Toward The Negro, 1550-1812*. Chapel Hill, NC: University of North Carolina Press.

Jung, C.C. (1953) The relationship between the ego and the unconscious. In *The Collected Works of C.G. Jung*, (7), Princeton, NJ: Princeton University Press.

Katz, D., Sarnoff, I., & McClintock, C. (1956) Ego-defense and attitude change. *Human Relations,* (9), 27-45.

Katz, I., Henchy, T., & Allen, H. (1968) Effects of race of tester, approval-disapproval, and need on Negro children's learning. *Journal of Personality and Social Psvchology,* (8), 38-42.

Katz, P.A., Sohn, M., & Zalk, S.R. (1974) Perceptual concomitants of racial attitudes in urban grade-school children. *Developmental Psychology.*

Katz, P.A. (1973) Stimulus predifferentiation and modification of children's racial attitudes. *Child Development,* (44), 232-237.

Katz, P.A., & Zalk, S.R. (1974) Doll preferences: An index of racial attitudes? *Journal of Educational Psychology,* (66), 663-668.

Katz, P.A., & Seavey, C. (1973) Labels and children's perception of faces. *Child Development,* (44), 770-775.

Katz, P.A. (1976) *Toward The Elimination of Rascism.* New York, NY: Pergamon Press.

Kerlinger, F.N. (1967) *Foundations of Behavioral Research.* New York, NY: Holt, Rinehart, and Winston.

Klineberg, 0. (1950) Tensions affecting international understanding. *Social Science Research Council Bulletin,* 62. New York, NY: Social Science Research Council.

Knowles, L., & Prewitt, K. (Eds.) (1969) *Institutional Racism In America.* Englewood Cliffs, NJ: Prentice-Hall.

Kovel, J. (1970). *White Racism: A Psychohistory.* New York, NY: Pantheon.

Kutash, I.L., Schlesinger, L.B., & Associates. (1980) *Handbook on Stress and Anxiety*. SanFrancisco. CA: Jossey-Bass Publishers.

Kutner, B. (1958) Patterns of mental functioning associated with prejudice in children. *Psychological Monographs*, (72), 1-48.

Levin H. (1960) *The Power of Blackness*. New York, NY: Vintage.

Levinson, D. (1950) The study of ethnocentric ideology. In Adorno, et al., *The Authoritarian Personality*. New York, NY: W.W. Norton.

Liebert, R.M., Sobol, M.R., & Copemann, C.D. (1972) Effects of vicarious consequences and race of model upon imitative performance by black children. *Developmental Psychology*, (6), 453-456.

Mann, H.J. (1959) The effects of inter-racial contact on sociometric choices and perceptions. *Journal of Social Psychology*, (59), 143-152.

Maykovitch, M.K. (1972) Reciprocity in racial stereotypes: white, black, and yellow. *American Journal of Sociology*, (77), 876-897.

McLean, H.V. (1946) Psychodynamic factors in racial relations. *The Annals of the American Academy of Political and Social Science*, (244), 159-166.

Mezei, L. (1971) Perceived social pressure as an explanation of shifts in relative influence of race and belief on prejudice across social interactions. *Journal of Personality and Social Psychology*, (19), 69-81.

Minard, R.D. (1952) Race relationships in the Pocahontas coal field. *Journal of Social Issues*, 8(1), 29-44.

Monte, C. (Ed.) (1977) *Beneath the Mask: An Introduction to Theories of Personality*. New York, NY: Praeger Publishers.

Morland, J.K. (1958) Racial recognition by nursery school children in Lychburg, Virginia. *Social Forces,* (37), 132-137.

Morton, C. (1839) *Crania Americana.* Philadelphia, PA: J. Dobson.

Morland, J.K. (1962) Racial acceptance and preference of nursery school children in a southern city. *Merrill-Palmer Quarterly,* (8), 271-280.

Morland, J.K. (1966) A comparison of race awareness in northern and southern children. *American Journal of Orthopsychiatry,* (36), 22-31.

Munn, N.L. (1961) *Psychology–The Fundamentals of Human Adjustment.* Boston, MA: Houghton Mifflin Company.

Murray, Henry A. (1963) *Explorations in Personality.* (7th ed.) New York, NY: Oxford University Press.

Nash, G. (1970) Red, white, and black: the origins of racism in colonial America. In G. Nash & R. Weiss (Eds.), *The Great Fear: Race in the Mind of America.* New York, NY: Holt, Rinehart, & Winston.

Nunnally, J. (1961) *Popular Conceptions of Mental Health.* New York, NY: Holt, Rinehart, & Winston.

Osgood, C.E., Suci, G.J., & Tannenbaum, P.H. (1968) *The Measurement of Meaning.* Urbana, IL: University of Illinois Press.

Palermo, D.S., & Jenkins, J.J. (1964) *Word Association Norms.* Minneapolis, MN: University of Minnesota Press.

Perlman, D., & Oskamp, S. (1971) The effects of picture content and exposure frequency on evaluations of Negroes and Whites. *Journal of Experimental Social Psychology,* (7), 503-514.

Pinderhughes, C.A. (1971, May). Racism: a paranoia with contrived reality and processed violence. Paper presented at the joint meeting of the American Psychiatric Association and the American Psychoanalytic Association, Washington, D.C.

Porter, J. (1971) *Black Child, White Child: Development o Racial Attitudes.* Cambridge, MA: Harvard University Press.

Pouissaint, A. (1974) Blaxploitation movies: cheap thrills that degrade blacks. *Psychology Today,* 7(9), 22-32, 98.

Proshansky, H. (1966) The development of intergroup attidues. In I.W. Hoffman & M.L. Hoffman (Eds), *Review of Child Development Research,* (2). New York, NY: Russell Sage Foundation.

Radke-Yarrow, M., Trager, H., & Miller, J. (1952) The role of parents in the development of children's ethnic attitudes. *Child Development,* (23), 13-53.

Rokeach, M. (1971) Long-range modification of values, attitudes, and behavior. *American Psychologist,* (26), 453-459.

Rosenblith, J.F. (1949) A replication of "some roots of prejudice." *Journal of Abnormal and Social Psychology,* (44), 470-489.

Rubin, I.M. (1967) Increased self-acceptance: A means of reducing prejudice. *Journal of Personality and Social Psychology,* (5), 233-238.

Sanford, R., et al. (1950). The measurement of implicit antidemocratic trends. In Adorno, et al., *The Authoritarian Personality.* New York, NY: W.W. Norton.

Sanford, R. N. (1950) The contrasting ideologies of two college men: a preliminary view. In Adorno, et al., *The Authoritarian Personality.* New York, NY: W.W. Norton.

Sears, D. O., & Kinder, D. R. (1971) Racial tensions and voting in Los Angeles (1970). In W.Z. Hirsch (Ed.), *Los Angeles: Viability and Prospects for Metropolitan Leadership* (51-58). New York, NY: Praeger.

Seidenberg, R. (1952) The sexual bias of social psychology. *Psychoanalytic Review*. (39). 90-95.

Seth-Roberts, J. (1972) *The Nature of Personal Reality*. Englewood Cliffs, NJ: Prentice-Hall, Inc.

Sherif, M. (1966) *In Common Predicament: Social Psychology of Intergroup Conflict and Cooperation*. Boston, MA: Houghton Mifflin Company.

Spielberger, C.D. (1975) Anxiety: state-trait process. In C.D. Spielberger & I.G. Sarason (Eds.), *Stress and Anxiety*, (1). New York, NY: Halsted Press.

Stotland, E., Katz, D., & Patchen, M. (1959) The reduction of prejudice through the arousal of self-insight. *Journal of Personality*, (27), 507-531.

Sullivan, H. S. (1953) *The Interpersonal Theory of Psychiatry*. New York, NY: W.W. Norton.

Tajfel, H., & Wilkes, A.L. (1963) Classification and quantitative judgment. *British Journal of Psychology*, (54), 101-114.

Tajfel, H., Sheikh, A.A., & Gardner, R.C. (1964) Content of stereotypes and the influence of similarity between members of stereotyped groups. *Acta Psychologia*, (22), 191-201.

Tajfel, H. (1969) Cognitive aspects of prejudice. *Journal of Social Issues*, (25), 79-97.

Tajfel, H. (1970) Experiments in intergroup discrimination. *Scientific American*, (233), 96-102.

Tajfel, H. (1973) The roots of prejudice: cognitive aspects. In P. Watson (Ed),
   Psychology and Race. Chicago, IL: Aldine.

Wadeson, R.W. (1971) Empathy: An antidote to individual racism. Paper
   presented at the joint meeting of the American Psychiatric Association and
   the American Psychoanalytic Association, Washington, D.C.

Walk, R.D. (1956) Self-ratings of fear in a fear-provoking situation. *Journal of
   Abnormal and Social Psychology,* (52), 171-178.

Weissbach, T.A. (1976) Laboratory controlled studies of change of racial attitudes.
   In P.A. Katz (Ed.), *Toward the Elimination of Racism.* New York, NY:
   Pergamon Press.

Williams, J.E. (1964) Connotations of color names among Negroes and
   Caucasians. *Perceptual and Motor Skills,* (18), 721-731.

Williams, J.E. (1965) Connotations of racial concepts and color names. *Journal of
   Personality and Social Psychology,* (3), 531-540.

Williams, J.E., & Renninger, C.A. (1966) Black-white color connotations and
   racial awareness in preschool children. *Perceptual and Motor Skills,* (22),
   771-785.

Williams, J.E., & Roberson, K.A. (1967) A method for assessing racial attitudes
   in preschool children. *Educational and Psychological Measurement,* (27),
   671-689.

Williams, J.E. (1972) Racial attitudes in preschool children: modification via
   operant conditioning, and a revised measurement procedure. Paper
   presented at the American Psychological Association, Honolulu.

Williams, J.E. (1973) Changes in the connotations of racial concept and color
   names: 1963-1970. *Psychological Reports,* 33(3), 983-996.

Williams, J.E. (1974) Preschool racial attitudes measure II. *Educational and Psychological Measurement.*

Williams, J.E., & Morland, J.K. (1976) *Race, Color, and The Young Child.* Chapel Hill, NC: University of North Carolina Press.

Williams, J.E., Tucker, R.D., & Dunham, F.Y. (1971) Changes in the connotations of color names among Negroes and Caucasians. *Journal of Personality and Social Psychology,* (19), 222-228.

Woodmansee, J. (1966) An evaluation of pupil response as a measure of attitude toward Negroes. *Dissertation Abstracts,* 26(11), 6897-6897.

Woodmansee, J.J., & Cook, S.W. (1967) Dimensions of verbal racial attitudes: Their identification and measurement. *Journal of Personality and Social Psychology,* (7), 240-250. (Woodmansee, 1965 included in study.)

Woodward, C.V. (1966) *Strange Career of Jim Crow.* New York, NY: Oxford University Press.

Zawadski, B. (1948) Limitations of the scapegoat theory of prejudice. *Journal of Abnormal and Social Psychology,* (43), 127-141.

Zuckerman, M. (1960) The development of an affect adjective checklist for the measurement of anxiety. *Journal of Consulting Psychology,* (24), 457-462.

APPENDIX

PACKAGE OF ACTIVITIES

NAME_____
I. D. CODE_____

    Enclosed is a series of _____ activities that are designed to get some
opinions, ideas, feelings, and impressions about different situations and items.
Please read carefully the instructions for each activity and then proceed with the
activity. It is important that you complete all activities in order and that you do no
skip any of the items or activities. The information that you provide will be dealth
with in such a way as to maintain confidentiality. We ask therefore that you
respond honestly and frankly to the items in the various activities.

    On the next page is a list of words. Please take a moment, read the
directions, and complete the brief task. Then, proceed quickly to Activity I.

I. D. CODE_____

Please check all the words below which describe you have felt <u>today</u>. "Today" here is defined as beginning from the time you awoke this morning up to the present moment.

Calm_____   Panicky_____
Cheerful_____   Shaky_____
Afraid_____   Pleasant_____
Contented____   Tense_____
Desperate____   Terrified_____
Fearful_____   Secure_____
Happy_____   Upset_____
Frightened___   Worrying_____
Joyful_____   Steady_____
Nervous_____   Thoughtful_____
Loving_____

Activity I

I. D. CODE_____

AGE_____   SEX_____

DIRECTIONS

In the following activity you are asked to compare your behavioral and emotional reactions with those of most men or women of your given sex and of your own age–with the respective hypothetical average among college men or women.

Read each statement carefully and make up your mind whether it is <u>more</u> or <u>less</u> true for you than it is for the average. Then, <u>make a check</u> in the proper column according to the following system:

<u>Below</u> <u>Average</u>

Column - (minus) 3 = I do, or I feel, or I think this thing <u>very much less</u> often (or intensely) thatn the average.

Column - (minus) 2 = I do, or I feel, or I think this thing <u>less</u> often (or intensely) than the average.

Column -(minus) 1 = average, but on the low side.

<u>Above</u> <u>Average</u>

Column + (plus) 1 = average, but on the high side.

Column + (plus) 2 = I do, or I feel, or I think this thing <u>more</u> often (or intensely) than the average.

Column + (plus) 3 = I do, or I feel, or I think this thing <u>very much more</u> often (or intensely) than the average.

<u>Do not skip any statement</u>. Each statement should have a check in a column appropriate to you.

		BELOW AVERAGE			ABOVE AVERAGE		
		-3	-2	-1	+1	+2	+3

1. I enjoy psychological novels more than other kinds of literature.

2. I believe that I have an instintive understanding of the underlying motives of people.

3. I enjoy an intimate conversation with one person more than a general conversation with several.

4. I feel that I know a good deal about my own motives and feelilngs.

5. I am more interested in a person's behavior than in his inner life.

6. In the molding of character I think that external conditions are more important than inner tendencies.

7. I am apt to become rather deeply and emotionally involved with one person or another.

8. I like to review in my mind the impressions which other people have made upon me.

9. I dislike morbid psychological novels.

10. I spend very little time worrying about problems of love and sex.

11. I like to work with mechanical appliances: machinery, electrical apparatus and so forth.

	BELOW AVERAGE			ABOVE AVERAGE		
	-3	-2	-1	+1	+2	+3

12. I enjoy scientific articles more than fiction or poetry.

13. I think that I have a fair understanding of women (or men).

14. I often think I can feel my way into the innermost being of another.

15. I am apt to judge people in terms of their accomplishments

16. I feel things deeply and personally, and am sensitive to the deeper feelings of others.

17. Mathematics has been one of my best subjects.

18. My fantasies are an important part of my life.

19. I am rather detached and impersonal in my dealings with other people.

20. In the conduct of my life I bother very little about practical details.

21. I often imagine myself accomplishing great deeds.

22. I feel that ideals are powerful motivating forces in myself and in others.

23. I am often at a loss to explain the behavior of people who are emotionally unstable.

24. I am practical and efficient when there is something to be done.

		BELOW AVERAGE			ABOVE AVERAGE		
		-3	-2	-1	+1	+2	+3

25. I am interested in the business and financial problems of the day.

26. I am interested in all kinds of new mechanical devices.

27. I like to dramatize events in which I am participating.

28. I usually see things as a whole; am apt to disregard minor details.

29. I live in my imagination as much as I do in the external world.

30. I believe in the value and importance of inner revelation.

31. I generalize freeely; am apt to make rather sweeping and exaggerated statements.

32. I am much more apt to think of an object's utility than of its symbolic value.

33. I stick to the unadorned facts when I tell about something that happened.

34. I rely as much on intuition or faith as I do on the results of past experience.

35. I spend very little time thinking about distant goals and ultimate ideals.

36. I work for tangible and clearly defined results.

37. I give my imagination free sway when I am thinking or talking.

	BELOW AVERAGE			ABOVE AVERAGE		
	-3	-2	-1	+1	+2	+3

38. I am thrilled by ideas which are large and all-embracing.

39. I am apt to see an underlying symbolic meaning in the stories that I read.

40. I find it rather easy to work out an effective, sober plan of action.

41. I accept the world as it is and do not try to imagine how it might be.

42. Some of my friends think that my ideas are impractical if not a bit wild.

43. Sometimes I think of natural objects as possessing human qualities.

44. I always attempt to substantiate the facts of a case before giving a judgement.

45. My anticipations remain within the realm of what is probable, i.e., they are based on past experience.

46. I am influential in the conduct of my life by a vision of my destiny.

47. I am temparamentally opposed to the "romantic" point of view.

48. I have a few, if any, emotional problems.

	BELOW AVERAGE			ABOVE AVERAGE		
	-3	-2	-1	+1	+2	+3

49. I often do things merely for my private emotional satisfaction, no matter whether anything is accomplished or not.

50. I feel that a person's life should be the full expression of his innermost self.

51. I often hope for a situation which will allow me to act out one of my fantansies.

52. I find it easy to think things out calmly without the interferences of sentiment.

53. I like to keep myself free from emotional entanglements.

54. I am apt to make up stories by myself about the private thoughts and experiences of the people whom I meet.

55. I act on the principle that a man's (or woman's) first duty is to adjust him/herself to his/her environment.

56. I have moods of expansive elation when I feel like embracing the whole world.

57. My hopes and expectations are very exuberant when I embark upon a new enterprise.

58. I am rathker moderate and judicious in my judgments of other people.

59. I am quite conventional in my behavior.

		BELOW AVERAGE			ABOVE AVERAGE		
		-3	-2	-1	+1	+2	+3
60.	My relations with other people are simple and uncomplicated.						
61.	I keep my feet on the ground, i.e., I adopt a common-sense and matter-of-fact attitude toward life.						
62.	I accept the verdict of my own feelings as the surest guide to what is right.						
63.	I have, at times, been utterly dejected by disillusionment.						
64.	My best thoughts often come at times of emotional stress.						
65.	I feel that the heart is as good a guide as the head.						
66.	I should say that my ideas were sound and sensible, rather than unusual or imaginative.						
67.	When I tackle a subject I read what others have written about it before I begin.						
68.	I like to associate with people who take life emotionally.						
69.	I am specifically interested in ideas that are thoroughly practical.						
70.	I believe that the economic interpretation of history is as valid as any.						
71.	Without zest and excitement life seems pale and shallow.						
72.	My head is full of ideas clamouring for expression.						

	BELOW AVERAGE			ABOVE AVERAGE		
	-3	-2	-1	+1	+2	+3
73. I believe that the world may be well lost for love.		I	I	II	I	I
74. I adopt a somewhat skeptical or agnostic point of view towards most theories.		I	I	II	I	I
75. It is easier for me to deal with concrete facts in one special field than with general ideas about man or nature.		I	I	II	I	I
76. I am rather "tough-minded" or "hard-boiled" in my interpretations and judgments.		I	I	II	I	I
77. I think more about my private feelings or theories than I do about the practical demands of everyday existance.		I	I	II	I	I
78. I dislike everything that has to do with money–buying, selling, and bargaining.		I	I	II	I	I
79. I am inclined towards a mechanistic (or materialistic) conception of nature.		I	I	II	I	I
80. I believe that science offers as good a guide as there is to the future.		I	I	II	I	I
81. I would rather write a find book than be an important public figure.		I	I	II	I	I
82. When I think out a problem I keep very close to the facts.		I	I	II	I	I
83. I can deal with an actual situation better than I can cope with general ideas and theories.		I	I	II	I	I

BELOW AVERAGE			ABOVE AVERAGE		
-3	-2	-1	+1	+2	+3

84. I am a practical person, interested in tangible achievements.

85. I would rather grow inwardly and achieve balance and fullness of experience than win success in practical affairs.

86. I have a rather good head for business.

87. I like being in the thick of action.

88. I am interested in everything that is going on in the world: business, politics, social affairs, etc.

89. I would rather take an active part in contemporary events than read and think about them.

90. I am extremely interested in the activities of other people.

91. I like to do things with my hands: manual labor, manipulation or construction.

92. I like above all to discuss general questions–scientific or philosophical–with my friends.

93. I am apt to brood for a long time over a single idea.

94. I like to have people about me most of the time.

95. I am more interested in aesthetic or moral values than I am in contemporary events.

		BELOW AVERAGE			ABOVE AVERAGE		
		-3	-2	-1	+1	+2	+3
96.	Money and social prestige are matters of importance to me.		I	I	II	I	I
97.	I am inclined to withdraw from the world of restless action.		I	I	II	I	I
98.	I would rather <u>know</u> than <u>do</u>.		I	I	II	I	I
99.	I spend a lot of time philoso-phizing with myself.		I	I	II	I	I
100.	When I hear a person speak, I think more about his person-ality than I do about what he is saying.		I	I	II	I	I

Activity II

DIRECTIONS

The purpose of this exercise is to measure the meanings of certain items to various people by having them judge them against a series of descriptive scales. Please make your judgments on the basis of what these items mean to you. On each page you will find a different concept to be judged and beneath it a set of scales. The following is an example:

CARS

good   __ : __ : __ : __ : __ : __ __   bad

ugly   __ : __ : __ : __ : __ : __ : __   pretty

You are to rate the concept on each of these scales in order, as shown above. The direction toward which you check, of course, depends upon which of the two ends of the scale seems most characteristic of the item you're judging. Sometimes you may feel as though you've had the same item before. This will not be the case, so do not look back and forth through the items. Do not try to remember how you checked similar items earlier. There will be several items that contain the word "unconscious", however. For our purposes, "unconscious" here refers to the parts or portions of the self that one generally is not consciously aware of–the inner, more subjective, not readily conscious parts of the self. Nevertheless, make each item a separate and independent judgment. Work as rapidly as you can and don't worry or puzzle over individual items. It is your first impression, the immediate "feelings" about the item that we want. On the otherhand, please do not be careless, because we want your true impressions. Do not skip any items. Now turn the page and go ahead. Work fast.

The Nature of Life

dirty	:	:	:	:	:	:	clean
sacred	:	:	:	:	:	:	profane
active	:	:	:	:	:	:	passive
strong	:	:	:	:	:	:	weak
mysterious	:	:	:	:	:	:	understandable
powerless	:	:	:	:	:	:	powerful
relaxed	:	:	:	:	:	:	tense
strange	:	:	:	:	:	:	familiar
civilized	:	:	:	:	:	:	primitive
chaotic	:	:	:	:	:	:	organized
good	:	:	:	:	:	:	bad
dark	:	:	:	:	:	:	bright
frightening	:	:	:	:	:	:	nonfrightening

The Nature of the Unconscious

dirty _____:_____:_____:_____:_____:_____clean

sacred _____:_____:_____:_____:_____:_____profane

active _____:_____:_____:_____:_____:_____passive

strong _____:_____:_____:_____:_____:_____weak

mysterious___:_____:_____:_____:_____:_____understandable

powerless___:_____:_____:_____:_____:_____powerful

relaxed_____:_____:_____:_____:_____:_____tense

strange_____:_____:_____:_____:_____:_____familiar

civilized_____:_____:_____:_____:_____:_____primitive

chaotic_____:_____:_____:_____:_____:_____organized

good _____:_____:_____:_____:_____:_____bad

dark _____:_____:_____:_____:_____:_____bright

frightening___:_____:_____:_____:_____:_____nonfrightening

The Nature of Consciousness

dirty _____:_____:_____:_____:_____:_____:_____clean

sacred _____:_____:_____:_____:_____:_____:_____profane

active _____:_____:_____:_____:_____:_____:_____passive

strong _____:_____:_____:_____:_____:_____:_____weak

mysterious___:_____:_____:_____:_____:_____:_____understandable

powerless____:_____:_____:_____:_____:_____:_____powerful

relaxed_____:_____:_____:_____:_____:_____:_____tense

strange_____:_____:_____:_____:_____:_____:_____familiar

civilized____:_____:_____:_____:_____:_____:_____primitive

chaotic_____:_____:_____:_____:_____:_____:_____organized

good _____:_____:_____:_____:_____:_____:_____bad

dark _____:_____:_____:_____:_____:_____:_____bright

frightening___:_____:_____:_____:_____:_____:_____nonfrightening

The Nature of the Waking State During the Day

dirty _____:_____:_____:_____:_____:_____:_____clean

sacred _____:_____:_____:_____:_____:_____:_____profane

active _____:_____:_____:_____:_____:_____:_____passive

strong _____:_____:_____:_____:_____:_____:_____weak

mysterious____:_____:_____:_____:_____:_____:_____understandable

powerless____:_____:_____:_____:_____:_____:_____powerful

relaxed_____:_____:_____:_____:_____:_____:_____tense

strange_____:_____:_____:_____:_____:_____:_____familiar

civilized_____:_____:_____:_____:_____:_____:_____primitive

chaotic_____:_____:_____:_____:_____:_____:_____organized

good _____:_____:_____:_____:_____:_____:_____bad

dark _____:_____:_____:_____:_____:_____:_____bright

frightening____:_____:_____:_____:_____:_____:_____nonfrightening

The Unknown

dirty _____:_____:_____:_____:_____:_____:_____clean

sacred _____:_____:_____:_____:_____:_____:_____profane

active _____:_____:_____:_____:_____:_____:_____passive

strong _____:_____:_____:_____:_____:_____:_____weak

mysterious___:_____:_____:_____:_____:_____:_____understandable

powerless___:_____:_____:_____:_____:_____:_____powerful

relaxed___:_____:_____:_____:_____:_____:_____tense

strange___:_____:_____:_____:_____:_____:_____familiar

civilized___:_____:_____:_____:_____:_____:_____primitive

chaotic___:_____:_____:_____:_____:_____:_____organized

good _____:_____:_____:_____:_____:_____:_____bad

dark _____:_____:_____:_____:_____:_____:_____bright

frightening___:_____:_____:_____:_____:_____:_____nonfrightening

The Nature of Satan

dirty	:	:	:	:	:	:	clean
sacred	:	:	:	:	:	:	profane
active	:	:	:	:	:	:	passive
strong	:	:	:	:	:	:	weak
mysterious	:	:	:	:	:	:	understandable
powerless	:	:	:	:	:	:	powerful
relaxed	:	:	:	:	:	:	tense
strange	:	:	:	:	:	:	familiar
civilized	:	:	:	:	:	:	primitive
chaotic	:	:	:	:	:	:	organized
good	:	:	:	:	:	:	bad
dark	:	:	:	:	:	:	bright
frightening	:	:	:	:	:	:	nonfrightening

The Black Race

dirty _____:_____:_____:_____:_____:_____:_____clean

sacred _____:_____:_____:_____:_____:_____:_____profane

active _____:_____:_____:_____:_____:_____:_____passive

strong _____:_____:_____:_____:_____:_____:_____weak

mysterious___:_____:_____:_____:_____:_____:_____understandable

powerless___:_____:_____:_____:_____:_____:_____powerful

relaxed_____:_____:_____:_____:_____:_____:_____tense

strange_____:_____:_____:_____:_____:_____:_____familiar

civilized_____:_____:_____:_____:_____:_____:_____primitive

chaotic_____:_____:_____:_____:_____:_____:_____organized

good _____:_____:_____:_____:_____:_____:_____bad

dark _____:_____:_____:_____:_____:_____:_____bright

frightening___:_____:_____:_____:_____:_____:_____nonfrightening

The Nature of Death

dirty _____:_____:_____:_____:_____:_____:_____clean

sacred_____:_____:_____:_____:_____:_____:_____profane

active_____:_____:_____:_____:_____:_____:_____passive

strong_____:_____:_____:_____:_____:_____:_____weak

mysterious___:_____:_____:_____:_____:_____:_____understandable

powerless___:_____:_____:_____:_____:_____:_____powerful

relaxed_____:_____:_____:_____:_____:_____:_____tense

strange_____:_____:_____:_____:_____:_____:_____familiar

civilized____:_____:_____:_____:_____:_____:_____primitive

chaotic_____:_____:_____:_____:_____:_____:_____organized

good _____:_____:_____:_____:_____:_____:_____bad

dark _____:_____:_____:_____:_____:_____:_____bright

frightening__:_____:_____:_____:_____:_____:_____nonfrightening

White

dirty	:	:	:	:	:	:	clean
sacred	:	:	:	:	:	:	profane
active	:	:	:	:	:	:	passive
strong	:	:	:	:	:	:	weak
mysterious	:	:	:	:	:	:	understandable
powerless	:	:	:	:	:	:	powerful
relaxed	:	:	:	:	:	:	tense
strange	:	:	:	:	:	:	familiar
civilized	:	:	:	:	:	:	primitive
chaotic	:	:	:	:	:	:	organized
good	:	:	:	:	:	:	bad
dark	:	:	:	:	:	:	bright
frightening	:	:	:	:	:	:	nonfrightening

The White Race

dirty	:	:	:	:	:	:	clean
sacred	:	:	:	:	:	:	profane
active	:	:	:	:	:	:	passive
strong	:	:	:	:	:	:	weak
mysterious	:	:	:	:	:	:	understandable
powerless	:	:	:	:	:	:	powerful
relaxed	:	:	:	:	:	:	tense
strange	:	:	:	:	:	:	familiar
civilized	:	:	:	:	:	:	primitive
chaotic	:	:	:	:	:	:	organized
good	:	:	:	:	:	:	bad
dark	:	:	:	:	:	:	bright
frightening	:	:	:	:	:	:	nonfrightening

Red

dirty	:	:	:	:	:	:	clean
sacred	:	:	:	:	:	:	profane
active	:	:	:	:	:	:	passive
strong	:	:	:	:	:	:	weak
mysterious	:	:	:	:	:	:	understandable
powerless	:	:	:	:	:	:	powerful
relaxed	:	:	:	:	:	:	tense
strange	:	:	:	:	:	:	familiar
civilized	:	:	:	:	:	:	primitive
chaotic	:	:	:	:	:	:	organized
good	:	:	:	:	:	:	bad
dark	:	:	:	:	:	:	bright
frightening	:	:	:	:	:	:	nonfrightening

Friend

dirty	:	:	:	:	:	:	clean
sacred	:	:	:	:	:	:	profane
active	:	:	:	:	:	:	passive
strong	:	:	:	:	:	:	weak
mysterious	:	:	:	:	:	:	understandable
powerless	:	:	:	:	:	:	powerful
relaxed	:	:	:	:	:	:	tense
strange	:	:	:	:	:	:	familiar
civilized	:	:	:	:	:	:	primitive
chaotic	:	:	:	:	:	:	organized
good	:	:	:	:	:	:	bad
dark	:	:	:	:	:	:	bright
frightening	:	:	:	:	:	:	nonfrightening

Black

dirty _____:_____:_____:_____:_____:_____:_____clean
sacred _____:_____:_____:_____:_____:_____:_____profane
active _____:_____:_____:_____:_____:_____:_____passive
strong _____:_____:_____:_____:_____:_____:_____weak
mysterious___:_____:_____:_____:_____:_____:_____understandable
powerless___:_____:_____:_____:_____:_____:_____powerful
relaxed____:_____:_____:_____:_____:_____:_____tense
strange____:_____:_____:_____:_____:_____:_____familiar
civilized____:_____:_____:_____:_____:_____:_____primitive
chaotic____:_____:_____:_____:_____:_____:_____organized
good _____:_____:_____:_____:_____:_____:_____bad
dark _____:_____:_____:_____:_____:_____:_____bright
frightening___:_____:_____:_____:_____:_____:_____nonfrightening

People

dirty _____:_____:_____:_____:_____:_____:_____clean

sacred _____:_____:_____:_____:_____:_____:_____profane

active _____:_____:_____:_____:_____:_____:_____passive

strong _____:_____:_____:_____:_____:_____:_____weak

mysterious_____:_____:_____:_____:_____:_____:_____understandable

powerless_____:_____:_____:_____:_____:_____:_____powerful

relaxed_____:_____:_____:_____:_____:_____:_____tense

strange_____:_____:_____:_____:_____:_____:_____familiar

civilized_____:_____:_____:_____:_____:_____:_____primitive

chaotic_____:_____:_____:_____:_____:_____:_____organized

good _____:_____:_____:_____:_____:_____:_____bad

dark _____:_____:_____:_____:_____:_____:_____bright

frightening_____:_____:_____:_____:_____:_____:_____nonfrightening

The Nature of the Dreaming State During the Night

dirty   _____ : _____ : _____ : _____ : _____ : _____ clean

sacred _____ : _____ : _____ : _____ : _____ : _____ profane

active _____ : _____ : _____ : _____ : _____ : _____ passive

strong _____ : _____ : _____ : _____ : _____ : _____ weak

mysterious _____ : _____ : _____ : _____ : _____ : _____ understandable

powerless _____ : _____ : _____ : _____ : _____ : _____ powerful

relaxed _____ : _____ : _____ : _____ : _____ : _____ tense

strange _____ : _____ : _____ : _____ : _____ : _____ familiar

civilized _____ : _____ : _____ : _____ : _____ : _____ primitive

chaotic _____ : _____ : _____ : _____ : _____ : _____ organized

good   _____ : _____ : _____ : _____ : _____ : _____ bad

dark   _____ : _____ : _____ : _____ : _____ : _____ bright

frightening _____ : _____ : _____ : _____ : _____ : _____ nonfrightening

The Nature of the Unconscious Portions of the Self

dirty	:	:	:	:	:	:	clean
sacred	:	:	:	:	:	:	profane
active	:	:	:	:	:	:	passive
strong	:	:	:	:	:	:	weak
mysterious	:	:	:	:	:	:	understandable
powerless	:	:	:	:	:	:	powerful
relaxed	:	:	:	:	:	:	tense
strange	:	:	:	:	:	:	familiar
civilized	:	:	:	:	:	:	primitive
chaotic	:	:	:	:	:	:	organized
good	:	:	:	:	:	:	bad
dark	:	:	:	:	:	:	bright
frightening	:	:	:	:	:	:	nonfrightening

Yellow

dirty	:	:	:	:	:	:	clean
sacred	:	:	:	:	:	:	profane
active	:	:	:	:	:	:	passive
strong	:	:	:	:	:	:	weak
mysterious	:	:	:	:	:	:	understandable
powerless	:	:	:	:	:	:	powerful
relaxed	:	:	:	:	:	:	tense
strange	:	:	:	:	:	:	familiar
civilized	:	:	:	:	:	:	primitive
chaotic	:	:	:	:	:	:	organized
good	:	:	:	:	:	:	bad
dark	:	:	:	:	:	:	bright
frightening	:	:	:	:	:	:	nonfrightening

Enemy

dirty   :   :   :   :   :   :   clean
sacred   :   :   :   :   :   :   profane
active   :   :   :   :   :   :   passive
strong   :   :   :   :   :   :   weak
mysterious   :   :   :   :   :   :   understandable
powerless   :   :   :   :   :   :   powerful
relaxed   :   :   :   :   :   :   tense
strange   :   :   :   :   :   :   familiar
civilized   :   :   :   :   :   :   primitive
chaotic   :   :   :   :   :   :   organized
good   :   :   :   :   :   :   bad
dark   :   :   :   :   :   :   bright
frightening :   :   :   :   :   :   nonfrightening

The Nature of the Unconscious Portions of Me

dirty _____ : _____ : _____ : _____ : _____ : _____ clean
sacred _____ : _____ : _____ : _____ : _____ : _____ profane
active _____ : _____ : _____ : _____ : _____ : _____ passive
strong _____ : _____ : _____ : _____ : _____ : _____ weak
mysterious _____ : _____ : _____ : _____ : _____ : _____ understandable
powerless _____ : _____ : _____ : _____ : _____ : _____ powerful
relaxed _____ : _____ : _____ : _____ : _____ : _____ tense
strange _____ : _____ : _____ : _____ : _____ : _____ familiar
civilized _____ : _____ : _____ : _____ : _____ : _____ primitive
chaotic _____ : _____ : _____ : _____ : _____ : _____ organized
good _____ : _____ : _____ : _____ : _____ : _____ bad
dark _____ : _____ : _____ : _____ : _____ : _____ bright
frightening _____ : _____ : _____ : _____ : _____ : _____ nonfrightening

Brown

dirty _____:_____:_____:_____:_____:_____:_____clean

sacred _____:_____:_____:_____:_____:_____:_____profane

active _____:_____:_____:_____:_____:_____:_____passive

strong _____:_____:_____:_____:_____:_____:_____weak

mysterious_____:_____:_____:_____:_____:_____:_____understandable

powerless_____:_____:_____:_____:_____:_____:_____powerful

relaxed_____:_____:_____:_____:_____:_____:_____tense

strange_____:_____:_____:_____:_____:_____:_____familiar

civilized_____:_____:_____:_____:_____:_____:_____primitive

chaotic_____:_____:_____:_____:_____:_____:_____organized

good _____:_____:_____:_____:_____:_____:_____bad

dark _____:_____:_____:_____:_____:_____:_____bright

frightening_____:_____:_____:_____:_____:_____:_____nonfrightening

The Nature of God

dirty	:	:	:	:	:	:	clean
sacred	:	:	:	:	:	:	profane
active	:	:	:	:	:	:	passive
strong	:	:	:	:	:	:	weak
mysterious	:	:	:	:	:	:	understandable
powerless	:	:	:	:	:	:	powerful
relaxed	:	:	:	:	:	:	tense
strange	:	:	:	:	:	:	familiar
civilized	:	:	:	:	:	:	primitive
chaotic	:	:	:	:	:	:	organized
good	:	:	:	:	:	:	bad
dark	:	:	:	:	:	:	bright
frightening	:	:	:	:	:	:	nonfrightening

Activity III

OPINION INVENTORY

Here are some questions we are asking respondents attending college. Please give your own <u>honest opinion</u>.

<u>Do not put your name on this booklet.</u>

This booklet contains numbered statements. Read each statement carefully. If you agree with it more than you disagree, check under "A" (agree) on the Answer Sheet. If you disagree with it more than you agree, check under "D" (disagree).

<u>Do not leave any blanks.</u> <u>Please answer every statement.</u>

<u>Be sure</u> that the number of the statement agrees with the number of your answer sheet. The Answer Sheet is enclosed.

Before and after the set of questions on the Opinion Inventory, you will find a scale (or scales). Take a moment, read the directions, and complete the brief task both immediately before and immediately upon finishing the activity.

Now turn the page and go ahead. <u>Work fast.</u>

SCALE

Please place a check mark beside the appropriate number which indicates your level of anxiety for this experience. On the 1–to–10 scale below, 10 represents the highest level.

10	_____
9	_____
8	_____
7	_____
6	_____
5	_____
4	_____
3	_____
2	_____
1	_____

ANSWER SHEET
OPINION INVENTORY

CHECK: "A" <u>if you agree</u>   I. D. CODE_____
              "B" <u>if you disagree</u>   _____

	A	D		A	D		A	D		A	D		A	D
1.	( )	( )	21.	( )	( )	41.	( )	( )	61.	( )	( )	81.	( )	( )
2.	( )	( )	22.	( )	( )	42.	( )	( )	62.	( )	( )	82.	( )	( )
3.	( )	( )	23.	( )	( )	43.	( )	( )	63.	( )	( )	83.	( )	( )
4.	( )	( )	24.	( )	( )	44.	( )	( )	64.	( )	( )	84.	( )	( )
5.	( )	( )	25.	( )	( )	45.	( )	( )	65.	( )	( )	85.	( )	( )
6.	( )	( )	26.	( )	( )	46.	( )	( )	66.	( )	( )	86.	( )	( )
7.	( )	( )	27.	( )	( )	47.	( )	( )	67.	( )	( )	87.	( )	( )
8.	( )	( )	28.	( )	( )	48.	( )	( )	68.	( )	( )	88.	( )	( )
9.	( )	( )	29.	( )	( )	49.	( )	( )	69.	( )	( )	89.	( )	( )
10.	( )	( )	30.	( )	( )	50.	( )	( )	70.	( )	( )	90.	( )	( )
11.	( )	( )	31.	( )	( )	51.	( )	( )	71.	( )	( )	91.	( )	( )
12.	( )	( )	32.	( )	( )	52.	( )	( )	72.	( )	( )	92.	( )	( )
13.	( )	( )	33.	( )	( )	53.	( )	( )	73.	( )	( )	93.	( )	( )
14.	( )	( )	34.	( )	( )	54.	( )	( )	74.	( )	( )	94.	( )	( )
15.	( )	( )	35.	( )	( )	55.	( )	( )	75.	( )	( )	95.	( )	( )
16.	( )	( )	36.	( )	( )	56.	( )	( )	76.	( )	( )	96.	( )	( )
17.	( )	( )	37.	( )	( )	57.	( )	( )	77.	( )	( )	97.	( )	( )
18.	( )	( )	38.	( )	( )	58.	( )	( )	78.	( )	( )	98.	( )	( )
19.	( )	( )	39.	( )	( )	59.	( )	( )	79.	( )	( )	99.	( )	( )
20.	( )	( )	40.	( )	( )	60.	( )	( )	80.	( )	( )	100.	( )	( )

Do Not Write In This Space:

INSE ACPT BINF INCON SUDB LAUT PRRT STSUP GRAD BSUP

___ _____ ___ _____ ____ ____ ____ _____ ____ ____

DO NOT MAKE ANY MARKS ON THIS BOOKLET

---

1. Black people should be accorded equal rights through affirmative programs for integration.

2. I would have no worries about going to a party with an attractive Black date.

3. I would accept an invitation to a New Year's Eve party given by a Black couple in their own home.

4. There is nothing to the idea tht the Black man's troubles in the past have built in him a stronger character than the White man has.

5. I think it is right that the Black race should occupy a somewhat lower position socially than the White race.

6. Despite civil rights laws, a hotel owner ought to have the right to decide for himself whether he is going to rent rooms to Black guests.

7. The Black and the White man are inherently equal.

8. There should be a strictly enforced law requiring bussing to achieve school desegregation regardless of race, creed or color.

9. Blacks sometimes imagine they have been discriminated against on the basis of color even when they have been treated quite fairly.

10. If I were a teacher, I would not mind at all taking advice from a Black principal.

11. In a local community or campus charity drive I would rather not be represented by a Black chairperson even if he or she were qualified for the job.

12. Society has a moral right to insist that a community desegregate even if it doesn't want to.

13. Gradual desegregation without such efforts as affirmative action programs or quota systems is a mistake because it just gives people a chance to cause further delay.

14. School officials should not be trying to place Black and White children in the same schools because of the danger of fights and other problems.

15. I probably would feel somewhat self-conscious dancing with a Black in a public place.

16. Despite civil rights laws, the people of each state should be allowed to decide for or against integration efforts in state matters (e.g., bussing for school desegregation).

17. It is better to work gradually toward fuller integration without such efforts as affirmative action programs or quota systems than to try to bring it about all at once.

18. I think that Blacks have a kind of quiet courage which few White people have.

19. I would not take a Black person to eat with me in a restaurant where I was well known.

20. Some Blacks are so touchy about getting or maintaining their rights that it is difficult to get along with them.

21. A person should not have the right to run a business in this country if s/he will not do business with Blacks.

22. I would rather not have Blacks swim in the same pool as I do.

23. Affirmative Action Officers should be supported in their efforts to force acceptance of desegregation through affirmative action.

24. Those who advise patience and "slow down" in affirmative actions or continued desegregtion are wrong.

25. I favor gradual rather than sudden changes in the social relations between Blacks and Whites.

26. I can easily imagine myself falling in love with and marrying a Black.

27. Suffering and trouble have made Blacks better able to withstand the stresses and strains of modern life than most Whites.

28. Even without the civil right laws, I believe that the Black man is entitled to the same social privileges as the White man.

29. I am willing to have Blacks as close personal friends.

30. There is no basis in fact for the idea that Blacks withstand misfortune more courageously than do most Whites.

31. We should not integrate housing until Black people raise their standards of living.

32. Many Blacks should receive better education than they are now getting, but the emphasis should be on training them for jobs rather than preparing them for college.

GO ON TO THE NEXT PAGE

33.   Barbers and beauticians have the right to refuse service to anyone they please, even if it means refusing Blacks.

34.   Although social equality of the races may be the democratic way, a good many Blacks are still not yet ready to practice the self-control that goes with it.

35.   If I were being interviewed for a job, I would not mind at all being evaluated by a Black personnel director.

36.   It would be a mistake ever to have Blacks for foremen and leaders over Whites.

37.   Many Blacks spend money for big cars and television sets instead of spending it for better housing.

38.   I would feel somewhat uneasy talking about intermarriage with Blacks whom I do not know well.

39.   Fuller integration and access through affirmative action efforts will result in greater understanding between Blacks and Whites.

40.   Since we live in a democracy, if we don't want fuller integration it should not be forced upon us.

41.   I would not mind at all if my only friends were Blacks.

42.   There should be a law requiring persons who take roomers in their homes to rent to anyone regardless of race, creed, or color.

43.   In fields where they have been given an opportunity to advance, Blacks have shown that they are good sports and gentlemen.

44.   I would willingly go to a competent Black surgeon.

45.   It is not right to ask Americans to accept integration (for example, in housing & education) if they honestly don't believe in it.

46.   I feel that moderation will do more for increased desegregation than the efforts of Affirmative Action Officers to force it immediately on people.

47.   Blacks should be given every opportunity to get ahead, but they could never be capable of holding or accepted for top leadership positions in this country (e.g., President of the United States).

48.   If a Black person is qualified for an executive job, s/he should get it, even if it means that s/he will be supervising highly educated White persons.

GO ON TO THE NEXT PAGE

49. If I were eating lunch in a restaurant alone with a Black person, I would be less self-conscious if the Black person were of the same sex as I rather than the opposite sex.

50. Even if there were complete equality of opportunity tomorrow, it would still take a long time for Blacks to show themselves equal to Whites in some areas of life.

51. Fuller integration of the schools will be beneficial to both White and Black children alike.

52. There is no reason to believe that what Blacks have suffered in the past has made them a more noble people than are Whites.

53. I would rather not have Blacks as dinner guests with most of my White friends.

54. I think that Black people have a sense of dignity that you see in few White people.

55. If I were a business man, I would resent it if I were told that I had to do business with Blacks.

56. Local communities should have no right to delay the further desegregation of their community facilities, agencies, etc.

57. In the long run continued desegregation would go more smoothly if we put it into effect immediately.

58. Fuller integration should not be attempted because of the turmoil it causes.

59. Even if Blacks are given increased opportunity for college education, it will be several generations before they are ready to take advantage of it.

60. The fact that Blacks are human beings can be recognized without raising them to the current social level of Whites.

61. There is nothing to the idea that Blacks have more sympathy for other minorities than most Whites do.

62. I have no objection to attending the movies or a play in the company of a Black couple.

63. The inability of Black people to develop outstanding leaders restricts them to a low place in society.

64. Fuller integration is more trouble than it is worth.

GO ON TO THE NEXT PAGE

65.   It doesn't work to force further desegregation on a community before it is ready for it.

66.   The history of Black people in America shows that the process of gradual integration of the races is much too slow.

67.   If further desegregation is pushed too fast, Black people's cause will be hurt rather than helped.

68.   Real estate agents should be required, if they are not currently, to show homes to Black buyers regardless of the desires of home owners.

69.   Despite civil rights laws, if I were a landlord, I would want to pick my own tenants even if this meant renting only to Whites.

70.   Even though Black people may have some cause for complaint, they would get what they want faster if they were a bit more patient about it.

71.   I feel in sympathy with responsible Blacks who are fighting for affirmative action programs for desegregation purposes.

72.   Most Blacks really think and feel the same way most Whites do.

73.   In this day of rush and hurry, the Black man has met the problems of society in a much calmer manner than the White man.

74.   Before I sponsored a Black person for membership in an all White club, I would think a lot about how this would make the other members feel toward me.

75.   If I were invited to be a guest of a mixed Black and White group on a weekend pleasure trip, I would probably not go.

76.   If the Blacks were of the same social class level as I am, I'd just as soon move into a Black neighborhood as a White one.

77.   I would rather not serve on the staff of a Black congressman.

78.   The problem of racial injustice has been greatly exaggerated by a few Black agitators.

79.   If he were qualified, I would be willing to vote for a Black person for President of the United States.

80.   Many favored a more moderate policy, but I believe that during the 1960's civil rights period Black people should have been encouraged to picket and sit in at places where they were not treated fairly.

GO ON TO THE NEXT PAGE

81. Desegregation laws often violate the rights of the individual who does not want to associate with Blacks.

82. There is no basis in fact for the idea that the Black person's misfortunes have made him/her a more understanding person than the average White.

83. Since segregation has been declared illegal, we should integrate schools in actuality.

84. I'd be willing to consult a Black lawyer.

85. I would rather not have Blacks live in the same apartment building I live in.

86. I would be willing to introduce Black visitors to friends and neighbors in my home town.

87. The Black person's own experience with unfair treatment has given him/her a sensitivity and understanding that will make him/her an excellent supervisor of White people.

88. The best way to integrate the schools more fully is to do it all at once.

89. People who don't have to live with problems of race relations have no right to dictate to those who do.

90. If I were working on a community or campus problem with somebody, I would rather it not be a Black person.

91. When I see a Black person and a White person together as a couple, I'm inclined to be more curious about their relationship than if they were both Black or both White.

92. It is a good idea to have separate schools for Blacks and Whites to avoid forced bussing.

93. Race discrimination is not just a local community's problem, but one which often demands action from those outside the community.

94. I have as much respect for some Black persons as I do for some White persons, but the average Black and I share little in common.

95. It makes no difference to me whether I'm Black or White.

96. Regardless of his own views, an employer should continue to be required to hire workers without regard to race.

GO ON TO THE NEXT PAGE

97.   Although social mixing of the races may be rith in principle, it is impractical until Blacks learn to accept more "don'ts" in relations between teenage boys and girls.

98.   I could trust a Black person as easily as I could trust a White person if I know him/her well enough.

99.   School integration should have begun with the first few grades rather than all grades at once.

100.   If I were a Black person, I would not want to gain entry into places where I was not really wanted.

SCALES

Please place a check mark beside the appropriate numbers which indicate your level of anxiety <u>during</u> the experience and for <u>now</u> <u>after</u> the experience. On the 1–to–10 scale below, 10 represents the highest level.

<u>DURING</u>   <u>NOW (AFTER)</u>

10 _____   10 _____

9 _____   9 _____

8 _____   8 _____

7 _____   7 _____

6 _____   6 _____

5 _____   5 _____

4 _____   4 _____

3 _____   3 _____

2 _____   2 _____

1 _____   1 _____

Activity IV

INSTRUCTIONS: Please circle for each item the word that most nearly describes the amount of fear that you feel toward the object or situation noted in the item.

1.   Sharp Objects
a. None
b. Very little
c. A little
d. Some
e. Much
f. Very much
g. Terror

6.   Looking Foolish
a. None
b. Very little
c. A little
d. Some
e. Much
f. Very much
g. Terror

2.   Being a Passenger in a Car

a. None
b. Very little
c. A little
d. Some
e. Much
f. Very much
g. Terror

7.   Being a Passenger in an plane
a. None
b. Very little
c. A little
d. Some
e. Much
f. Very much
g. Terror

3.   Dead Bodies
a. None
b. Very little
c. A little
d. Some
e. Much
f. Very much
g. Terror

8.   Worms
a. None
b. Very little
c. A little
d. Some
e. Much
f. Very much
g. Terror

4.   Suffocating
a. None
b. Very little
c. A little
d. Some
e. Much
f. Very much
g. Terror

9.   Arguing with Parents
a. None
b. Very little
c. A little
d. Some
e. Much
f. Very much
g. Terror

5.   Failing a Test
a. None
b. Very little
c. A little
d. Some
e. Much
f. Very much
g. Terror

10.   Rats and Mice
a. None
b. Very little
c. A little
d. Some
e. Much
f. Very much
g. Terror

11. Life after Death
   a. None
   b. Very little
   c. A little
   d.Some
   e. Much
   f. Very much
   g. Terror

12. Hyperdermic Needles
   a. None
   b. Very little
   c. A little
   d. Some
   e. Much
   f. Very much
   g. Terror

13. Being Criticized
   a. None
   b. Very little
   c. A little
   d. Some
   e. Much
   f. Very much
   g. Terror

14. Meeting Someone for the First Time
   a. None
   b. Very little
   c. A little
   d. Some
   e. Much
   f. Very much
   g. Terror

15. Roller Coasters
   a. None
   b. Very little
   c. A little
   d. Some
   e. Much
   f. Very much
   g. Terror

16. Being Alone
   a. None
   b. Very little
   c. A little
   d. Some
   e. Much
   f. Very much
   g. Terror

17. Making Mistakes
   a. None
   b. Very little
   c. A little
   d. Some
   e. Much
   f. Very much
   g. Terror

18. Being Misunderstood
   a. None
   b. Very little
   c. A little
   d. Some
   e. Much
   f. Very much
   g. Terror

19. Death
   a. None
   b. Very little
   c. A little
   d. Some
   e. Much
   f. Very much
   g. Terror

20. Being in a Fight
   a. None
   b. Very little
   c. A little
   d. Some
   e. Much
   f. Very much
   g. Terror

21.   Crowded Places
      a. None
      b. Very little
      c. A little
      d. Some
      e. Much
      f. Very much
      g. Terror

22.   Blood
      a. None
      b. Very little
      c. A little
      d. Some
      e. Much
      f. Very much
      g. Terror

23.   Heights

      a. None
      b. Very little
      c. A little
      d. Some
      e. Much
      f. Very much
      g. Terror

24.   Being a Leader
      a. None
      b. Very little
      c. A little
      d. Some
      e. Much
      f. Very much
      g. Terror

25.   Swimming Alone
      a. None
      b. Very little
      c. A little
      d. Some
      e. Much
      f. Very much
      g. Terror

26.   Illness
      a. None
      b. Very little
      c. A little
      d. Some
      e. Much
      f. Very much
      g. Terror

27.   Being with Drunks
      a. None
      b. Very little
      c. A little
      d. Some
      e. Much
      f. Very much
      g. Terror

28.   Illness or Injury to Loved
      Ones
      a. None
      b. Very little
      c. A little
      d. Some
      e. Much
      f. Very much
      g. Terror

29.   Being Self-conscious
      a. None
      b. Very little
      c. A little
      d. Some
      e. Much
      f. Very much
      g. Terror

30.   Driving a Car
      a. None
      b. Very little
      c. A little
      d. Some
      e. Much
      f. Very
      g. Terror

31. Meeting Authority
    a. None
    b. Very little
    c. A little
    d. Some
    e. Much
    f. Very much
    g. Terror

32. Mental Illness
    a. None
    b. Very little
    c. A little
    d. Some
    e. Much
    f. Very much
    g. Terror

33. Closed Places
    a. None
    b. Very little
    c. A little
    d. Some
    e. Much
    f. Very much
    g. Terror

34. Boating
    a. None
    b. Very little
    c. A little
    d. Some
    e. Much
    f. Very much
    g. Terror

35. Spiders
    a. None
    b. Very little
    c. A little
    d. Some
    e. Much
    f. Very much
    g. Terror

36. Thunderstorms
    a. None
    b. Very little
    c. A little
    d. Some
    e. Much
    f. Very much
    g. Terror

37. Not Being a Success
    a. None
    b. Very little
    c. A little
    d. Some
    e. Much
    f. Very much
    g. Terror

38. God
    a. None
    b. Very little
    c. A little
    d. Some
    e. Much
    f. Very much
    g. Terror

39. Snakes
    a. None
    b. Very little
    c. A little
    d. Some
    e. Much
    f. Very much
    g. Terror

40. Cemeteries
    a. None
    b. Very little
    c. A little
    d. Some
    e. Much
    f. Very much
    g. Terror

41.   Speaking Before a Group
      a. None
      b. Very little
      c. A little
      d. Some
      e. Much
      f. Very much
      g. Terror

42.   Seeing a Fight

      a. None
      b. Very little
      c. A little
      d. Some
      e. Much
      f. Very much
      g. Terror

43.   Death of a Loved One
      a. None
      b. Very little
      c. A little
      d. Some
      e. Much
      f. Very much
      g. Terror

44.   Dark Places
      a. None
      b. Very little
      c. A little
      d. Some
      e. Much
      f. Very much
      g. Terror

45.   Strange Dogs
      a. None
      b. Very little
      c. A little
      d. Some
      e. Much
      f. Very much
      g. Terror

46.   Deep Water
      a. None
      b. Very little
      c. A little
      d. Some
      e. Much
      f. Very much
      g. Terror

47.   Being with a Member of the
      Opposite Sex
      a. None
      b. Very little
      c. A little
      d. Some
      e. Much
      f. Very much
      g. Terror

48.   Stinging Insects
      a. None
      b. Very little
      c. A little
      d. Some
      e. Much
      f. Very much
      g. Terror

49.   Untimely or Early Death
      a. None
      b. Very little
      c. A little
      d. Some
      e. Much
      f. Very much
      g. Terror

50.   Losing a Job
      a. None
      b. Very little
      c. A little
      d. Some
      e. Much
      f. Very much
      g. Terror

51. Auto Accidents
    a. None
    b. Very little
    c. A little
    d. Some
    e. Much
    f. Very much
    g. Terror

Activity V

INSTRUCTIONS: Following are a couple of open-ended questions to which we would like you to respond. There are no right or wrong answers, so please respond to both questions with whatever thoughts, feelings, or impressions that occur to you.

1.   We all have times when we feel below par. What moods or feelings are the most unpleasant or disturbing to you?

2.   There is hardly a person who hasn't said to himself, "If this keeps up, I'll go nuts!" What might drive a person nuts?

Activity VI

INSTRUCTIONS: In the following exercise, you will be asked to use your imagination to write brief stories. Please read carefully the topics for the stories that you will be provided and then let your imagination help you to develop the story. Four topics will be provided and you should take about 10 minutes to complete the writing of the stories. You might find it useful to work with first impressions that come to you after reading the topic for a particular story. Now turn the page and go ahead.

Write a <u>brief</u> story involving a person as the boss of employees. In your story, describe what is going on, what the people might be <u>doing</u>, <u>feeling</u>, and <u>thinking</u> and how the story ends.

Write a <u>brief</u> story involving a couple. In your story, describe what is going on, what the people might be <u>doing</u>, <u>feeling</u>, and <u>thinking</u> and how the story ends.

Write a <u>brief</u> story involving a Black person as the boss of White employees. In your story, describe what is going on, what the people might be <u>doing</u>, <u>feeling</u>, and <u>thinking</u> and how the story ends.

Write a <u>brief</u> story involving a Black-White interracial couple. In your story, describe what is going on, what the people might be <u>doing</u>, <u>feeling</u>, and <u>thinking</u> amd how the story ends.

INSTRUCTIONS: Now that you have completed the writling of the four stories we'd like you to honestly assess your level of anxiety both <u>During</u> and upon completing (<u>After</u>) the writing of each story. If it would be helpful to you to refer back to what you have written, please do so. However, it is your feelings both during and immediately following the completion of a particular story that we want. So, if you do look back, do not alter the content but rather use it to help you better assess your level of anxiety both during and after the writing of a particular story. Place a check mark beside the appropriate numbers on the following scales.

	STORY 1		STORY 2	
	DURING	AFTER	DURING	AFTER
	10___	10___	10___	10___
	9 ___	9 ___	9 ___	9 ___
	8 ___	8 ___	8 ___	8 ___
	7 ___	7 ___	7 ___	7 ___
	6 ___	6 ___	6 ___	6 ___
	5 ___	5 ___	5 ___	5 ___
	4 ___	4 ___	4 ___	4 ___
	3 ___	3 ___	3 ___	3 ___
	2 ___	2 ___	2 ___	2 ___
	1 ___	1 ___	1 ___	1 ___

	STORY 3		STORY 4	
	DURING	AFTER	DURING	AFTER
	10___	10___	10___	10___
	9 ___	9 ___	9 ___	9 ___
	8 ___	8 ___	8 ___	8 ___
	7 ___	7 ___	7 ___	7 ___
	6 ___	6 ___	6 ___	6 ___
	5 ___	5 ___	5 ___	5 ___
	4 ___	4 ___	4 ___	4 ___
	3 ___	3 ___	3 ___	3 ___
	2 ___	2 ___	2 ___	2 ___
	1 ___	1 ___	1 ___	1 ___

BACKGROUND DATA FORM

Sex: M   F

I. D.   CODE _____

Race and/or Ethnic

Religious Preference if any

_____

_____

DIRECTIONS: Please give answers to each of the following questions. Be honest.

1.   Would you say that you are generally: (Please check one only.)
( ) very open to looking at yourself
( ) somewhat open to looking at yourself
( ) sometimes open and sometimes closed to looking at yourself
( ) somewhat closed to looking at yourself
( ) very closed to looking at yourself
( ) don't know

2.   Do you remember many of your dreams? (Please circle.)   Yes   No
a.   If yes, please check those items that apply:
( ) I think many of my dreams are clear and instructive to me
( ) I think many of my dreams are often confusing and make little sense
( ) I pay little attention to many of my dreams
( ) I don't know what to think about many of my dreams
( ) I tend to have (or did have) recurring dreams
( ) I have experienced nightmares more than once

3.   Do you believe that intuitions and hunches are important? (Please circle.)
Yes   No
a.   I consider myself to be more a(n):   (Please check one only.)
( ) thinking type person
( ) feeling type person
( ) intuitive type person
( ) sensation type person

4.   Do you believe that the self has both conscious and unconscious portions?
(Please circle.)   Yes   No
a.   Please explain briefly:

5.   Have you ever had any <u>prolonged</u> contact(s) or relationship(s) with a
person(s) from another race. (Please circle.)   Yes   No
a.   If yes, please indicate the race of the person, length of contact (i.e.,
less than 1 year; 1-3 years; 4-6 years; 7-9 years; 10-12 years; more than 12
years), and the nature of the contact(s) (i.e., intimate; family; friend;
acquaintance; if other, please explain).

<u>Race of Person</u>   <u>Length of Contact</u>   <u>Nature of Contact</u>

6.   On the average, how long do you tend to sleep at night? (Please check
one.)
( ) 3 hours   ( ) 4 hours   ( ) 5 hours   ( ) 6 hours   ( ) 7 hours
( ) 8 hours   ( ) 9 hours   ( ) 10 hours   ( ) more than 10 hours

7.   What is your individual and family income? Please check the appropriate
box for each category. Guess if you don't know.
a.   Individual Income   b.   Family Income (Parents)
( ) 0–$6,999   ( ) 0–$6,999
( ) $7000–$15,999   ( ) $7000–$15,999
( ) $16,000–$24,999   ( ) $16,000–$24,999
( ) $25,000–$34,999   ( ) $25,000–$34,999
( ) $35,000 & Above   ( ) $35,000 & Above

8.   Do you attend church, synagogue, a place of worship, etc.?
(Please check one.)
( ) Regularly (at least once a week or more)
( ) Often (at least twice a month)
( ) Occasionally (on & off sporadically during a year)
( ) Rarely (once in awhile over a prolonged period or only for special
        occasions)
( ) Not at all

9.   Which one of the following would you consider yourself? (Please check
one only.)
( ) Lower Class
( ) Working Class
( ) Lower Middle Class
( ) Middle Class
( ) Upper Middle Class
( ) Upper Class
( ) None of the above

10.   Do you work either full or part-time?   Yes   No   (If yes, please underline which one.)
       a.   If you are working, what is your occupation_____
       b.   If you are not working, what is/are the occupations of your parents
             (or guardians)_____

11.   Would you say that your religious beliefs are: (Check one)
       ( ) Very strong
       ( ) Strong
       ( ) Somewhat strong
       ( ) Not at all strong
       ( ) Don't know
       ( ) Does not apply to me

12.   Would you say that your religious beliefs guide you in your everyday behaviors toward others:
       ( ) To a very great extent
       ( ) Most of the time
       ( ) Sometimes they do; sometimes they don't
       ( ) Hardly at all
       ( ) Don't know
       ( ) Does not apply to me

Index